★★★★★

# GREAT FLAVORS

## CONCENTRATES

# COOKBOOK

FLAVOR ENHANCING RECIPES FROM AWARD WINNING CHEFS
THAT WILL TURN ORDINARY SAUCES AND MEALS
INTO EXTRAORDINARY CULINARY CREATIONS

A COLLECTION OF RECIPES BY BOB WARDEN
WITH GEORGE STELLA *&* JOHN COLAVITA

# GREAT
# FLAVORS
## STOCKS·SAUCES·SPICES
★★★★★
*"Ordinary becomes Extraordinary"*

• • • • •

Published by Great Flavors LLC

First paperback edition 2011

A collection of recipes by Bob Warden
with George Stella & John Colavita

Art Direction & Book design: Alexa Rae Barbiche

Photography: Julie Ann Coney, Chicago & Georgia Ditzler, Bucks County

• • • • •

Manufactured in the USA

ISBN 978-0-578-08727-6

# CONTENTS

ORDINARY TO EXTRAORDINARY
QUICK TIPS,
IDEAS & TERMINOLOGY...1

★★★★★

SAUCES & GRAVIES...4

SOUPS & STEWS...20

BEEF...34

POULTRY...48

PORK...58

VEAL & LAMB...66

SEAFOOD...74

BEANS & LEGUMES...82

VEGETABLES & SIDE DISHES...89

RICE & RISOTTO...98

PASTA...107

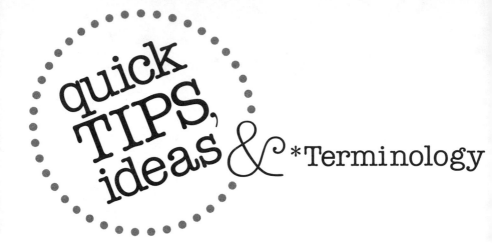

## Instant Pan Sauces

To make a delicious instant pan sauce, remove the cooked meat and/or browned vegetables and set aside, deglaze the cooking pan by stirring in 1 cup of wine and 1 teaspoon of the appropriate Great Flavors Concentrate. Variations can include; added mushrooms, shallots or onions, garlic, herbs and spices. For a richer pan sauce, you can finish by stirring in butter or heavy cream. You also may substitute water for the wine.

## Vegetable Secret

Add 1 teaspoon of Great Flavors Vegetable Concentrate to your steaming or boiling water. Mashed potatoes boiled in vegetable water are fantastic! Wait until you taste the difference!

## Instant Au Jus

Extend or make your own instant au jus by adding 2 teaspoons of Great Flavors Beef Concentrate to 1 cup of hot water. Or you can add this instant au jus* to extend the au jus collected from roasting.

## Easy, Instant Gravies

Mix 2 Tablespoons of flour with 2 Tablespoons of butter to make an uncooked roux*. Dissolve 2 teaspoons of Great Flavors Concentrate in one cup of hot water. Deglaze* cooking pan with the Concentrate mixture, and add the roux*. Stir over medium heat until the gravy thickens. Season with pepper to taste. Milk or cream can be substituted for the water for an even richer gravy.

## For Better Baked Beans

Add 1/2 teaspoon of Great Flavors Beef Concentrate to your favorite baked bean recipe, or 1/4 teaspoon to a 15.5 ounce can of prepared beans.

## Kick Your Meatloaf Up A Notch

Add 1 teaspoon of Great Flavors Beef Concentrate to the meatloaf egg filling mixture. You will not have to add additional salt.

## Seafood

When you are poaching fish add 1 teaspoon of Great Flavors Vegetable or Seafood Concentrate per 1 cup of poaching or water for steaming.

## Rice, Pasta, and Beans

Give any of these staples cooked in boiling water a flavor boost by adding 1 teaspoon of Great Flavors Vegetable or Chicken Concentrate to the cooking water.

## Scrambles Eggs, Omelets and French Toast

Give your eggs and omelets some extra zest and flavor by adding 1/4 teaspoon of Great Flavors Vegetable or Chicken Concentrate to every 2 eggs when preparing omelets, scrambled eggs and French toast.

## Mashed Potato Wow!

To kick your mashed potatoes up a notch add 2 teaspoons of Great Flavors Vegetable Concentrate for every 2 pounds of potatoes stirred into the milk or cream before whipping into potatoes.

## Pan Stuffing

Add 2 teaspoons Great Flavors Chicken Concentrate to your favorite stuffing recipe, and it will taste like it was cooked inside the bird!

## French Fry Secret

Yes, the secret to those special fast food fries is the addition of beef flavoring. To make yours taste just like your favorite, soak raw, sliced potatoes in 2 tablespoons of Great Flavors Beef Concentrate dissolved in water. Chill overnight in the refrigerator.
Be sure to drain and dry potatoes thoroughly before frying.

# *Terminology

## Roux (ROO)

A mixture of flour and fat that, after being slowly cooked over low heat, is used to thicken mixtures such as soups and sauces. There are three classic roux — white, blond and brown. The color and flavor is determined by the length of time the mixture is cooked. Both white roux and blond roux are made with butter. The former is cooked just until it begins to turn beige and the latter until pale golden. Both are used to thicken cream and white sauces and light soups. The fuller-flavored brown roux can be made with butter, drippings or pork or beef fat. It's cooked to a deep golden brown and used for rich, dark soups and sauces.

## Au Jus (oh-ZHOO)

A French phrase describing meat served with its own natural juices, commonly used with beef.

## Espagnole (ehs-pah-NYOHL)

Also referred to as Brown Sauce, it is known in France as "espagnole sauce", and is used as a base for dozens of other sauces. It's traditionally made of a rich meat stock, a mirepoix of browned vegetables, a brown roux, herbs and sometimes tomato paste.

## Julienne (joo-lee-EHN)

Foods that have been cut into thin, matchstick (very thin) strips approximately 1/8-inch-thick.

## Gremolata (greh-moh-LAH-tah)

A garnish made of minced parsley, lemon peel and garlic. It is often sprinkled over Osso Buco and other dishes to add a fresh, sprightly flavor.

## De Glaze (dee-GLAYZ)

To swirl or stir a liquid (usually wine or stock) in a pan to dissolve cooked food particles remaining on the bottom; the resulting mixture often becomes the base for a sauce. After food (usually meat) has been sautéed and the food and excess fat removed from the pan, deglazing is done by heating a small amount of liquid in the pan and stirring to loosen browned bits of food on the bottom.

## Slurry

A thin paste of water and flour, which is stirred into hot preparations (such as soups, stews and sauces) as a thickener. After the slurry is added, the mixture should be stirred and cooked for several minutes in order for the flour to lose its raw taste.

## Chiffonade (shihf-uh-NAHD)

Literally translated, this French phrase means "made of rags." Culinarily, it refers to thin strips or shreds of vegetables (classically, sorrel and lettuce), either lightly sautéed or used raw to garnish soups.

# SAUCES
# & GRAVIES

# Fresh Salsa

**YIELD: 5 CUPS**

## Ingredient List:

4 CUPS CHOPPED PEELED FRESH TOMATOES
1/4 CUP ONION, FINELY CHOPPED
1 JALAPENO PEPPER, SEEDED AND FINELY CHOPPED
1/4 CUP FRESH CILANTRO, CHOPPED
1 TABLESPOON FRESH SQUEEZED LIME JUICE
1 TEASPOON VEGETABLE CONCENTRATE
1 TEASPOON SALT
1 TEASPOON SUGAR
1 GARLIC CLOVE, MINCED
SALT AND PEPPER TO TASTE

## Instructions:

In a bowl, combine all ingredients; mix well. Let stand for about 1 hour.
Serve at room temperature.

# Fresh Tomato Sauce

**YIELD: 4 QUARTS**

## Ingredient List:

8 POUNDS TOMATOES, SEEDED AND DICED
3 TABLESPOONS VEGETABLE CONCENTRATE
1/4 CUP CHOPPED FRESH BASIL
1/2 POUND CARROTS, PUREED
1 LARGE ONION, MINCED
3 CLOVES GARLIC, MINCED
1/2 CUP OLIVE OIL
SALT AND PEPPER TO TASTE

## Instructions:

In large stockpot, cook tomatoes, Vegetable Concentrate, carrots and
basil over medium-low heat until tomatoes are soft. Meanwhile, in medium
skillet, sauté onion and garlic in olive oil until onions are translucent.
Add onion mixture to tomato mixture and add salt and pepper.
Let simmer on low heat for 2 hours or until thickened.

# Demi-Glace

*Great by itself or as a base for quick reduction sauces,*
*Demi-Glace is as rich in the history of French cooking as it is in flavor!*
*Traditionally made mixing the 'Mother Sauce" espagnole\* with carrots,*
*celery, onions and veal stock and then thickened with roux\*, the Veal*
*or Beef Concentrate used here has done it all for you!*

**PREP TIME: 10 MINUTES**
**COOK TIME: 10 MINUTES**
**YIELD: ABOUT 16 OUNCES; 10 SERVINGS**

## Ingredient List:

2 CUPS WATER

1/2 CUP DRY RED WINE

1 TABLESPOON RED ONION, MINCED

1 TEASPOON FRESH CHOPPED TARRAGON — *may use 1/4 teaspoon dry*

4 TABLESPOONS VEAL OR BEEF CONCENTRATE

1/4 TEASPOON SALT

1/8 TEASPOON BLACK PEPPER

1 TABLESPOON BUTTER

2 TABLESPOONS FLOUR

## Cooking Instructions:

Place a small sauce pan over high heat, add all the ingredients except the
butter and flour and bring to a simmer.
While the sauce heats, melt the butter in a small sauté pan over medium heat
and whisk in the flour just until blended to make a white roux\*.
Remove from heat and reserve.
Once simmering use a whisk to vigorously stir in the roux\* and continue
cooking about 2 or 3 minutes more until sauce thickens enough to coat
a wooden spoon. Remove from heat and pour through a wire mesh strainer.
Just before serving hot, stir in 1 tablespoon of cold butter to add richness.

# TIP
*To make meatloaf gravy, leave out the wine for*
*a "Basic" brown sauce and then add sautéed mushrooms.*
*Because Demi-Glace is thickened with roux\*, unlike reduction sauces*
*it will keep refrigerated for a week and can be frozen longer.*
*You may also use cornstarch as directed to thicken this and most sauces.*

# Horseradish Demi-Glace

YIELD: ABOUT 16 OUNCES; 10 SERVINGS

## Ingredient List:

2 CUPS WATER

1/2 CUP DRY RED WINE

1 TABLESPOON RED ONION, MINCED

1 TEASPOON FRESH CHOPPED TARRAGON — *may use 1/4 teaspoon dry*

4 TABLESPOONS VEAL OR BEEF CONCENTRATE

1/4 TEASPOON SALT

1/8 TEASPOON BLACK PEPPER

1 TABLESPOON BUTTER

2 TABLESPOONS FLOUR

2 TEASPOONS FRESH GROUND HORSERADISH

## Cooking Instructions:

Place a small sauce pan over high heat, add all the ingredients except the butter and flour and bring to a simmer. While the sauce heats, melt the butter in a small sauté pan over medium heat and whisk in the flour just until blended to make a white roux*. Remove from heat and reserve.

Once simmering use a whisk to vigorously stir in the roux* and continue cooking about 2 or 3 minutes more until sauce thickens enough to coat a wooden spoon. Remove from heat and pour through a wire mesh strainer and stir in the horseradish. Just before serving hot, stir in 1 tablespoon of cold butter to add richness, if desired.

# Worcestershire Demi-Glace

*For this Demi-Glace you will use the same recipe as above for the Horseradish Demi-Glace but replace the Horseradish in the recipe for your favorite Worcestershire Sauce.*

# Madeira Wine Sauce

*For this Sauce you will use the same recipe as above for the Horseradish Demi-Glace but replace 1/2 cup of dry red wine in the recipe for 1/2 cup Madeira wine.*

# Mushroom Bordelaise

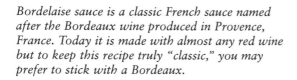

*Bordelaise sauce is a classic French sauce named after the Bordeaux wine produced in Provence, France. Today it is made with almost any red wine but to keep this recipe truly "classic," you may prefer to stick with a Bordeaux.*

## YIELD: ABOUT 8 OUNCES; 4 SERVINGS

## Ingredient List:

1 TABLESPOON OLIVE OIL

1 TEASPOON RED ONION, MINCED

1/2 CUP SLICED BUTTON MUSHROOMS

1/8 TEASPOON BLACK PEPPER

1/4 CUP BURGUNDY WINE — *may substitute any red wine*

1 TEASPOON CHOPPED FRESH TARRAGON — *may use 1/4 teaspoon dry*

1 TABLESPOON VEAL OR BEEF CONCENTRATE

1 TEASPOON MUSHROOM OR VEGETABLE CONCENTRATE

2 TABLESPOONS COLD BUTTER

## Cooking Instructions:

Place a large sauté pan over high heat and add the olive oil, onions, mushroom and pepper. Cook for just a minute until mushrooms are tender. Stir the wine, tarragon and Concentrates into the pan and continue cooking about 3 minutes to reduce until sauce lightly coats the back of a wooden spoon. Remove pan from heat and quickly stir in the cold butter by swirling the pan. Serve with steak, chicken, pasta, pork and more.

# TIP
*To turn this into a New Orleans Bordelaise sauce, add chopped garlic and parsley.*

# Cabernet Cream Sauce

**YIELD: ABOUT 6 OUNCES; 4 SERVINGS**

## Ingredient List:

1/4 CUP CABERNET WINE — *may substitute any red wine*

1 TABLESPOON RED ONION, MINCED

1 TEASPOON FRESH CHOPPED TARRAGON — *may use 1/4 teaspoon dry*

1/2 CUP HEAVY CREAM

1 TABLESPOON VEAL OR BEEF CONCENTRATE

## Cooking Instructions:

Place a large sauté pan over high heat and add the wine, onions and tarragon.
Cook for 2 minutes to reduce.
Stir cream and Concentrate into the pan and continue cooking for about
2 minutes more or until sauce has reduced enough to coat the back of
a wooden spoon. Serve with steak, veal, pork and more.

# Bordelaise Sauce

**YIELD: ABOUT 6 OUNCES; 4 SERVINGS**

## Ingredient List:

1/4 CUP BURGUNDY WINE — *may substitute any red wine*

1/8 TEASPOON BLACK PEPPER

1 TEASPOON MINCED RED ONION

1 SPRIG FRESH TARRAGON, CHOPPED — *may use 1/4 teaspoon dry*

1 TABLESPOON VEAL OR BEEF CONCENTRATE

2 TABLESPOONS COLD BUTTER

## Cooking Instructions:

Place a large sauté pan over high heat and add the wine, onions, and
tarragon and cook for about 2 minutes to reduce.
Stir Concentrate into the pan and continue cooking about 2 minutes more
until sauce lightly coats the back of a wooden spoon.
Remove pan from heat and quickly stir in the cold butter by swirling the pan.
Serve with steak, pasta, pork and more.

# Alfredo Sauce

YIELD: ABOUT 6 OUNCES; 4 SERVINGS

## Ingredient List:

1 CUP HEAVY CREAM
1 TEASPOON CHICKEN CONCENTRATE
1/4 CUP GRATED PARMESAN
1/8 TEASPOON SALT
1/8 TEASPOON PEPPER

## Cooking Instructions:

Place a large sauté pan over high heat, add all the ingredients and cook
while stirring for about 2 minutes to reduce until sauce lightly coats the back
of a wooden spoon. Quickly stir in the Parmesan cheese until melted.
Remove from heat and serve immediately with white fish or chicken.

# Amaretto Sauce

YIELD: ABOUT 4 OUNCES; 4 SERVINGS

## Ingredient List:

1/2 CUP HEAVY CREAM
1 TEASPOON CHICKEN CONCENTRATE
1 OUNCE AMARETTO LIQUOR — *may substitute 2 drops of Almond Extract*
1 TABLESPOON HONEY — *may substitute 1 teaspoon of sugar*
1 TABLESPOON DRY COCONUT FLAKES

## Cooking Instructions:

Place a large sauté pan over high heat, add all the ingredients and cook
while stirring for about 2 minutes to reduce until sauce lightly coats the back
of a wooden spoon. Remove from heat and serve immediately with
white fish or chicken.

# Béchamel Sauce

*Béchamel, or basic white sauce, is a neutral cream based sauce that instantly takes on the flavor of anything that is added to it. This is why most restaurants keep gallons of it on-hand.*

**PREP TIME: 5 MINUTES**
**COOK TIME: 10 MINUTES**
**YIELD: ABOUT 16 OUNCES; 10 SERVINGS**

## Ingredient List:

2 1/2 CUPS MILK

1 TABLESPOON CHICKEN CONCENTRATE

1/8 TEASPOON GRATED NUTMEG

1/8 TEASPOON SALT

1/8 TEASPOON WHITE PEPPER

1 TABLESPOON BUTTER

2 TABLESPOONS FLOUR

## Cooking Instructions:

Place a sauce pan over medium-high heat, add all the ingredients except the butter and flour and bring to a slow simmer.

While the milk heats, melt the butter in a small sauté pan over medium heat and whisk in the flour just until blended to create a white roux*.

Remove from heat and reserve.

Once milk is simmering, vigorously whisk in the roux* and continue stirring while cooking about 3 minutes more until sauce thickens enough to coat the back of a wooden spoon. Remove from heat and pour through a wire mesh strainer. Cool and refrigerate for up to a week.

# TIP

*Milk can easily burn so don't walk away from the stove.*

*&*

*If the sauce thickens when you reheat it,
simply thin with a little more milk or even water!*

# Vodka Sauce

*Vodka sauce is an Italian red sauce, plus cream and vodka.*
*It first gained popularity, when a variation won a national recipe*
*competition in Italy. It is the key ingredient in Penne alla Vodka.*

## YIELD: ABOUT 8 OUNCES; 4 SERVINGS

## Ingredient List:

1 TABLESPOON BUTTER

1/4 CUP DICED PROSCIUTTO — *may substitute ham*

1 CUP OF VODKA

1/2 CUP HEAVY CREAM

1/2 CUP TOMATO SAUCE

1 TABLESPOON CHICKEN CONCENTRATE

1/4 CUP GRATED PARMESAN CHEESE

1/8 TEASPOON SALT

1/8 TEASPOON PEPPER

## Cooking Instructions:

In a large sauté pan over medium-high heat, add the butter and prosciutto
(or ham) and cook for just a minute until browned.
Add the vodka, cream, tomato sauce and Chicken Concentrate.
Cook while stirring for about 2 minutes more to reduce until sauce
lightly coats the back of a wooden spoon.
Quickly stir in the Parmesan cheese just until melted.
Remove from heat and serve immediately with pasta, seafood and chicken.

# TIP

*You can make Vodka sauce with gin or white wine as well.*
*Alcohol is used because tomatoes have many flavor compounds that*
*are alcohol soluble. Vodka is traditional in commercial sauces*
*mainly because it is inexpensive.*

# Chicken Veloute

*Veloute is a versatile neutral water based sauce.*
*Restaurants are fond of it because it stores well and when needed can*
*be mixed 50-50 with cream, milk or most anything. An easy and inexpensive way*
*to make soups and sauces that can be kept hot for hours without separating.*

**PREP TIME: 5 MINUTES**
**COOK TIME: 10 MINUTES**
**YIELD: ABOUT 16 OUNCES; 10 SERVINGS**

## Ingredient List:

2 1/2 CUPS WATER

2 TABLESPOONS CHICKEN CONCENTRATE

1/8 TEASPOON SALT

1/8 TEASPOON WHITE PEPPER

1 TABLESPOON BUTTER

2 TABLESPOONS FLOUR

## Cooking Instructions:

Place a sauce pan over medium-high heat, add all the ingredients (except the
butter and flour) and bring to a slow simmer.
While the water heats, melt the butter in a small sauté pan over medium heat
and whisk in the flour just until blended to make a white roux*.
Remove from heat and reserve.
Once water is simmering, vigorously whisk in the roux* and continue stirring
while cooking about 3 minutes more until sauce thickens enough to coat
a wooden spoon. Remove from heat and pour through a wire mesh strainer.
Cool and store refrigerated for up to 2 weeks.

## TIP

*When using Veloute, remember to season and flavor well*
*as it is the most neutral of all French classic sauces with very little flavor.*
*It's really all about the stability, cost, long storage time*
*and ease of use that it offers.*

# Chablis Sauce

YIELD: ABOUT 16 OUNCES; 10 SERVINGS

## Ingredient List:

2 CUPS MILK
2 TABLESPOONS CHICKEN CONCENTRATE
1/2 CUP CHABLIS WINE — *may substitute any white wine*
1/8 TEASPOON SALT
1/4 TEASPOON BLACK PEPPER
1 TABLESPOON BUTTER
2 TABLESPOONS FLOUR

## Cooking Instructions:

Place a sauce pan over medium-high heat, add all the ingredients (except the butter and flour) and bring to a slow simmer. While the milk heats, melt the butter in a small sauté pan over medium heat and whisk in the flour just until blended. Remove from heat and reserve. Once simmering, vigorously whisk in the roux* and continue stirring while cooking about 3 minutes more until sauce thickens. Remove from heat and use to top lemon baked white fish or chicken breast.

# Easy Cheesy Sauce

YIELD: ABOUT 16 OUNCES; 10 SERVINGS

## Ingredient List:

2 CUPS MILK
2 TABLESPOONS CHICKEN CONCENTRATE
1/8 TEASPOON GROUND NUTMEG
1/8 TEASPOON SALT
1/4 TEASPOON BLACK PEPPER
1 TABLESPOON BUTTER
2 TABLESPOONS FLOUR
4 OUNCES AMERICAN CHEESE OR SMOKED GOUDA — *may substitute any cheese*

## Cooking Instructions:

Place a sauce pan over medium-high heat, add the milk, Chicken Concentrate, salt & pepper and bring to a slow simmer. While the milk heats, melt the butter in a small sauté pan over medium heat and whisk in the flour just until blended to make a white roux*. Remove from heat and reserve. Once simmering, vigorously whisk in the roux* and continue stirring while cooking about 3 minutes more until sauce thickens. Remove from heat and stir in the cheese until melted. Serve over chicken & vegetables or use as a starter for your favorite macaroni and cheese recipe.

# Creamy Dijon Sauce

YIELD: ABOUT 4 OUNCES; 2 SERVINGS

### Ingredient List:

1/2 CUP HEAVY CREAM

1 TEASPOON CHICKEN CONCENTRATE

1 TABLESPOON DIJON MUSTARD

1 TABLESPOON FRESH LEMON JUICE

1/8 TEASPOON SALT

1/8 TEASPOON PEPPER

### Cooking Instructions:

Place a large sauté pan over high heat, add all the ingredients and cook while stirring for about 2 minutes until sauce lightly coats the back of a wooden spoon. Serve immediately over fish or chicken.

# Creamy Dill Sauce

*For this Sauce you will use the same recipe as above for the Creamy Dijon Sauce but replace the Dijon mustard in the recipe for 1 tablespoon of fresh chopped dill — or you may use 1 teaspoon of dry dill.*

# Roasted Red Pepper Vinaigrette

YIELD: ABOUT 2 1/2 CUPS

### Ingredient List:

1 CUP ROASTED RED BELL PEPPERS

1/2 CUP OLIVE OIL

1/4 CUP RED WINE VINEGAR

2 TABLESPOONS VEGETABLE CONCENTRATE

2 TABLESPOONS PARMESAN CHEESE, GRATED

3 CLOVES GARLIC, CRUSHED

1/2 TEASPOON CHOPPED FRESH BASIL

1/4 CUP CHOPPED RED ONION

SALT AND PEPPER TO TASTE

Place peppers, oil, vinegar, Vegetable Concentrate, cheese, garlic, onion, basil and salt and pepper in blender; process until smooth. Refrigerate until ready to use.

# Au Poivre Sauce

**YIELD: ABOUT 6 OUNCES; 4 SERVINGS**

## Ingredient List:

1/4 CUP BURGUNDY WINE — *may substitute any red wine*

1 TABLESPOON RED ONION, MINCED

1 TEASPOON FRESH CHOPPED TARRAGON — *may use 1/4 teaspoon dry*

1/2 CUP HEAVY CREAM

1 TABLESPOON VEAL OR BEEF CONCENTRATE

1 TEASPOON CANNED GREEN PEPPERCORNS — *or 1/2 teaspoon whole black peppercorns*

## Cooking Instructions:

Place a large sauté pan over high heat and add the wine, onions and tarragon. Cook for 2 minutes to reduce. Stir cream, Concentrate and green peppercorns into the pan and continue cooking for about 2 minutes more or until sauce has reduced enough to coat the back of a wooden spoon. Serve with steak, veal, pork, chicken and more.

# Marsala Sauce

**YIELD: ABOUT 6 OUNCES; 4 SERVINGS**

## Ingredient List:

1/4 CUP MARSALA WINE

1 TABLESPOON RED ONION, MINCED

1 TEASPOON FRESH CHOPPED TARRAGON — *may use 1/4 teaspoon dry*

1/2 CUP HEAVY CREAM

1 TABLESPOON VEAL OR BEEF CONCENTRATE

1/2 TEASPOON FRESH CHOPPED PARSLEY

## Cooking Instructions:

Place a large sauté pan over high heat and add Marsala wine, onions and tarragon. Cook for 2 minutes to reduce. Stir cream and Concentrate into the pan and continue cooking for about 2 minutes more or until sauce lightly coats the back of a wooden spoon. Serve with chicken, steak, veal, pork, pasta and more.

# Beef Au Jus

YIELD: 4 1/4 CUPS

## Ingredient List:

4 CUPS WATER

3 TABLESPOONS BEEF CONCENTRATE

2 LARGE BAY LEAVES

1/4 TEASPOON SALT

1/4 TEASPOON BLACK PEPPER

## Cooking Instructions:

Add all the ingredients to a deep sauce pan over medium-high heat and bring to a simmer for 4 minutes; stirring frequently. Serve hot over sliced roast beef or on the side in a cup for dipping. Keeps refrigerated for up to 2 weeks.

# Brown Gravy

YIELD: ABOUT 4 CUPS

## Ingredient List:

6 TABLESPOONS BUTTER

6 TABLESPOONS FLOUR

1 TABLESPOON BEEF CONCENTRATE MIXED WITH 3 1/2 CUPS WATER

## Cooking Instructions:

In a medium sized skillet over medium heat, melt butter and stir in flour and whisk until smooth. Cook over medium high heat until golden brown.
Stir in the water and Beef Concentrate mix and cook stirring frequently until bubbly and it thickens to desired texture.

## TIP

*For a richer gravy, substitute milk for the water.*

# Chicken Gravy

**YIELD: 4 CUPS**

## Ingredient List:

6 TABLESPOONS BUTTER

6 TABLESPOONS FLOUR

1 TABLESPOON CHICKEN CONCENTRATE MIXED WITH 3 1/2 CUPS WATER

## Cooking Instructions:

In a medium sized skillet over medium heat, melt butter and stir in flour with a whisk until smooth. Cook over medium high heat until golden brown. Stir in the water and Chicken Concentrate mixture. Cook; stirring frequently until bubbly and it thickens to desired texture.

# TIP

*For a richer gravy, substitute milk for the water.*

# Holiday Turkey Gravy

**YIELD: 4 CUPS**

## Ingredient List:

6 TABLESPOONS BUTTER

6 TABLESPOONS FLOUR

1 CUP PAN DRIPPINGS FROM ROASTED TURKEY

1 TABLESPOON BEEF CONCENTRATE MIXED WITH 2 CUPS WATER.

1 CUP MILK

CHOPPED GIBLETS — *optional*

PEPPER TO TASTE

## Cooking Instructions:

In a medium sized skillet over medium heat, melt butter and stir in flour with a whisk until smooth. Cook over medium high heat until lightly browned. Stir in the milk, pan drippings, water and Beef Concentrate mix. Cook, stirring frequently until bubbly and it thickens to desired texture.

# SOUPS
# & STEWS

# Stracciatella Soup

*This old Italian natural "cold remedy" is best described as a cheesy version of a Chinese egg drop soup. Stracciatella is easier to make than it is to say and perfect on a cold morning or to prevent that cold!*

**PREP TIME: 5 MINUTES**
**COOK TIME: 10 MINUTES**
**SERVES: 6**

## Ingredient List:

6 CUPS WATER

4 TABLESPOONS CHICKEN CONCENTRATE

1/2 TEASPOON SALT — *more or less to taste*

1/4 TEASPOON BLACK PEPPER

1/4 CUP GRATED PARMESAN CHEESE

3 LARGE EGGS, BEATEN

2 TABLESPOONS FRESH PARSLEY, CHOPPED

## Cooking Instructions:

Add the water, Chicken Concentrate, salt and pepper to a saucepan and bring to a simmer. Add the Parmesan cheese and eggs to a bowl and beat with a fork to mix. Remove stock from heat, slowly add the eggs and cheese mixture and wait a few minutes for eggs to cook.
Stir before serving hot with chopped parsley on top.

# Black Bean Soup

*The cilantro is what really takes this soup to the next level.*
*It is similar in appearance to parsley, but definitely different in flavor.*
*Add cumin, chili powder and lime juice and you're eating black beans*
*as you'll swear they were always meant to be!*

PREP TIME: 10 MINUTES
COOK TIME: 35 MINUTES IN PRESSURE COOKER, 1 HOUR 15 MINUTES ON STOVETOP
SERVES: 6

## Ingredient List:

2 TABLESPOONS VEGETABLE OIL
1 TABLESPOON GARLIC, MINCED
1 STALK CELERY, CHOPPED SMALL
1 YELLOW ONION, DICED
1 RED BELL PEPPER, CHOPPED
1 POUND BLACK BEANS, UNCOOKED
4 TEASPOONS BEEF CONCENTRATE MIXED INTO 4 CUPS WARM WATER
1 CUP WATER
2 TABLESPOONS LIME JUICE
1 BAY LEAF
1 TABLESPOON FRESH CILANTRO, CHOPPED
1 TEASPOON CUMIN
1 TEASPOON CHILI POWDER
1 TABLESPOON LIGHT BROWN SUGAR
SALT AND PEPPER TO TASTE
SOUR CREAM FOR GARNISH — *optional*

## Cooking Instructions:

Heat oil, garlic, celery, onion and bell pepper in pressure cooker on brown or in
large saucepot on medium high for about 7 minutes, stirring frequently, until
onions are translucent. Rinse the dry black beans well and add to the pressure
cooker or saucepot. Cover with remaining ingredients (except for sour cream).
Set the pressure cooker to high, securely lock on the lid and cook for 35 minutes.
For stovetop cooking, bring to boil and simmer for 1 hour and 15 minutes.
When done remove lid and use a potato masher, or the back of a large serving
spoon to mash black beans against the bottom of the pressure cooker or saucepot
until two thirds of the beans are broken up, thickening the soup. You can also
use a slotted spoon to transfer two thirds of the beans to a food processor or
blender to puree and then add back into the soup. Salt and pepper to taste and
serve topped with sour cream.

# Mushroom Florentine Soup

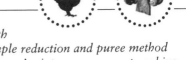

*Most soups today are heavy and thickened with
starches. No need for any of that with this simple reduction and puree method
that works well for almost any soup! Whether you're into easy gourmet cooking
or even low-carb, this classy cream of mushroom soup really fills the bill!*

PREP TIME: 10 MINUTES
COOK TIME: 10 MINUTES
SERVES: 2

## Ingredient List:

1 TABLESPOON BUTTER

8 OUNCES WHITE BUTTON MUSHROOMS, CLEANED AND SLICED

1 TEASPOON RED ONION, MINCED

1/4 TEASPOON SALT

1/4 TEASPOON BLACK PEPPER

2 1/2 CUPS WATER

1 TEASPOON MUSHROOM OR CHICKEN CONCENTRATE

1 CUP FRESH SPINACH LEAVES, WASHED AND STEMMED

1/2 CUP HEAVY CREAM, LEFT AT ROOM TEMPERATURE FOR 10 MINUTES

1 TEASPOON SOUR CREAM FOR GARNISH — *optional*

## Cooking Instructions:

Place a large sauté pan over medium-high heat and add the butter, mushrooms,
onions, salt and pepper. Cook while stirring for about 4 minutes until browned.
Add the water and Concentrate, turn the heat to high and cook for about
4 more minutes until reduced by half. Remove the pan from the heat; pour half
the soup into a blender cup and puree. Return the puree to the pan over high
heat and slowly stir in the spinach and cream to finish.
Serve in 2 soup bowls garnished with a dab of sour cream if desired.

# TIP

### LIGHTEN UP THIS RECIPE
*Replace the heavy cream with low-fat milk.
Simply dissolve 1 tablespoon of cornstarch into the water
before adding and it will thicken everything up!*

# Minestrone Soup with Tortellini

*Loosely translated from Italian, Minestrone means "The Big Soup"*
*for a reason. Though its ingredients have never been set in stone, one*
*thing has; it's fit to be a full meal. This take is certainly no different with spoon*
*after spoon of plump cheese stuffed tortellini: your family won't believe*
*it went from fridge to table in only 25 minutes!*

PREP TIME: 15MINUTES
COOK TIME: 5 MINUTES IN PRESSURE COOKER, 15 MINUTES ON THE STOVETOP
SERVES: 6

## Ingredient List:

2 TABLESPOONS OLIVE OIL
1 WHITE ONION, CHOPPED SMALL
2 STALKS CELERY, CUT INTO 1/4 INCH SLICES
2 CARROTS, SLICED INTO 1/4 INCH DISCS
1 TABLESPOON GARLIC, MINCED
8 OUNCE PACKAGE CHEESE TORTELLINI *(available in the regular dry goods pasta aisle)*
1 TABLESPOON VEGETABLE CONCENTRATE DISSOLVED IN 4 CUPS HOT WATER
1 JAR SPAGHETTI SAUCE (24-26 OUNCE)
1 CAN DICED TOMATOES (14.5 OUNCE)
1 1/2 TEASPOON ITALIAN SEASONING
1 TEASPOON SUGAR
1/4 TEASPOON GROUND BLACK PEPPER
SHREDDED PARMESAN CHEESE FOR GARNISH — *optional*

## Cooking Instructions:

Add the oil to the pressure cooker or large saucepot and heat on brown in
the pressure cooker or medium high heat on the stovetop. Sauté onions, celery,
carrots and garlic until onions begin to sweat, about 3 minutes.
Add the remaining ingredients and stir. For the pressure cooker securely
lock on the lid, set the cooker to high and cook for 5 minutes. For the stovetop
set heat to medium high, bring to boil, then reduce heat and simmer for
15 minutes or until tortellini is tender.
When done, serve topped with shredded or freshly grated Parmesan cheese.

# TIP

*These days there are plenty of varieties of jarred spaghetti sauces and dried*
*tortellini to choose from, so why not try making this recipe with a jar*
*of chunky mushroom tomato sauce or spinach tortellini or both!*

# Ground Beef Chili

*Make sure you have plenty of crackers on hand when preparing this wintertime classic. This legume free recipe is a terrific base to add a can or two of whichever beans you have in the pantry.*

**PREP TIME: 10 MINUTES**
**COOK TIME: 8 MINUTES IN PRESSURE COOKER, 16 TO 20 MINUTES ON STOVETOP**
**SERVES: 6**

## Ingredient List:

1 TABLESPOON VEGETABLE OIL
2 POUNDS LEAN GROUND BEEF
1 CUP ONION, CHOPPED LARGE
1 TABLESPOON GARLIC, MINCED
1 CAN DICED TOMATOES, WITH LIQUID (14 -16 OUNCES)
2 TEASPOONS CHICKEN CONCENTRATE MIXED INTO 2 CUPS OF WARM WATER
1 CAN MILD GREEN CHILI PEPPERS, WITH LIQUID (4 OUNCE)
1 TEASPOON SUGAR
1/2 TEASPOON CUMIN
2 TEASPOONS CHILI POWDER
2 TABLESPOONS CORNMEAL
SALT AND PEPPER TO TASTE
SHREDDED CHEDDAR CHEESE FOR GARNISH — *optional*

## Cooking Instructions:

Add the vegetable oil to a pressure cooker or large saucepot.
Set the pressure cooker to brown or the saucepot over medium high heat.
Add the ground beef, breaking it up with spoon or spatula as it browns.
Once the ground beef is browning well, add the chopped onion and minced garlic and stir in for 2 minutes. Add the remaining ingredients (except for cheddar cheese) and stir. For the pressure cooker, lock the lid and set the cooker to high and cook for 8 minutes. For the saucepot, set over medium high heat, bring to a simmer and cook for 16 to 20 minutes. When done, salt and pepper to taste and serve topped with shredded cheddar cheese.

# TIP

*Chili is a prime dish for all sorts of wonderful toppings. Shredded cheddar cheese goes without saying, but how about spicy pepper jack cheese? Sour cream, plain yogurt or even avocado can cool things down a bit. Chopped onions or even green onion tops can add a little flavor and crunch.*

# Cauliflower Soup

**PREP TIME: 5 MINUTES**
**COOK TIME: 30 MINUTES**
**SERVES: 4 TO 6**

### Ingredient List:

1 MEDIUM HEAD CAULIFLOWER, CHOPPED
1 SMALL ONION, CHOPPED
4 TEASPOONS CHICKEN CONCENTRATE MIXED WITH 4 CUPS OF HOT WATER
3/4 CUP OF RICE, UNCOOKED
1 CUP OF CREAM
SALT AND PEPPER TO TASTE

### Cooking Instructions:

In a large saucepot, combine 2 cups chicken broth mixture with cauliflower and
onion. Simmer until vegetables are very tender. Meanwhile, in another saucepot
add the rice to the remaining chicken stock and cook for 30 minutes.
Combine the two mixtures In a blender or food processor, puree until smooth,
adding cream as needed to achieve the desired consistency.
Salt and pepper to taste.

# Split Pea Soup

**PREP TIME: 5 MINUTES**
**COOK TIME: 30 MINUTES**
**SERVES: 4**

### Ingredient List:

4 TEASPOONS CHICKEN CONCENTRATE MIXED WITH 1 QUART OF HOT WATER
12 OUNCES OF DRIED SPLIT GREEN PEAS
1 SMALL ONION, CHOPPED
6 MEDIUM CARROTS, CHOPPED
1 STALK OF CELERY, CHOPPED
1/2 TEASPOON CUMIN
SALT AND PEPPER TO TASTE

### Cooking Instructions:

Combine all ingredients in a stockpot and simmer for about 45 minutes.
Blend in a food processor or blender until smooth. Add hot water if necessary
to achieve desired consistency. Salt and pepper to taste.

# Taco Soup

PREP TIME: 10 MINUTES
COOK TIME: 40 MINUTES
SERVES: 6 TO 8

## Ingredient List:

1 POUND GROUND BEEF

2 TABLESPOONS BEEF CONCENTRATE MIXED WITH 7 CUPS OF HOT WATER

1 CUP CELERY, DICED

2 CUPS POTATOES, DICED

2 CUPS ONIONS, DICED

1 CAN GREEN CHILI SALSA (7 OUNCES)

1 PACKAGE TACO SEASONING

2 CUPS DICED TOMATOES

1 CAN CONDENSED CHEDDAR CHEESE SOUP (10.75 OUNCES)

2 AVOCADOS, THINLY SLICED

SALT AND PEPPER TO TASTE

## Cooking Instructions:

In a small skillet, brown ground beef, stirring continuously and breaking into tiny pieces. Drain fat and set meat aside. In a large sauce pot combine beef stock mixture, celery, potatoes, and onions. Bring to a boil and simmer for 20 minutes. Add green chili salsa, taco seasonings, tomatoes, and cooked ground beef. Continue to simmer for 15 minutes. Add cheddar cheese soup and simmer for another 5 minutes stirring frequently to incorporate soup.
Salt and pepper to taste. Serve with a generous garnish of thinly sliced avocados.

# TIP

*To add complexity and texture to this soup,*
*add 1/2 cup each of sliced black and green olives.*

# Easy Prep Chicken with Rice Soup

PREP TIME: 2 MINUTES
COOK TIME: 25 MINUTES
SERVES: 4 TO 6

## Ingredient List:

3 TABLESPOONS CHICKEN CONCENTRATE MIXED WITH $1^{1/2}$ QUARTS OF HOT WATER
3/4 CUP WHITE RICE
1 - 12 OZ CAN OR 1 1/2 CUPS COOKED OR ROASTED CHICKEN, DICED
1 - 10 OUNCE PACKAGE OF FROZEN PEAS AND CARROTS
1 TEASPOON DRIED PARSLEY
SALT AND PEPPER TO TASTE

## Cooking Instructions:

In a medium saucepan, combine Chicken Concentrate mixture and rice.
Heat to boiling, reduce heat and simmer for 20 minutes or until rice is tender.
Add chicken, vegetables, parsley and salt & pepper to taste.
Return to simmer and cook for an additional 5 minutes.

# Simply Chicken Stew

PREP TIME: 10 MINUTES
COOK TIME: 2 HOURS
SERVES: 4 TO 6

## Ingredient List:

3 TO 4 POUNDS CHICKEN, CUT INTO CHUNKS
1 TABLESPOON VEGETABLE OIL
3 TEASPOONS CHICKEN CONCENTRATE MIXED WITH 3 CUPS OF HOT WATER
1 LARGE POTATO, CUBED
1 MEDIUM TURNIP, CUBED
2 MEDIUM CARROTS, CUBED
1 MEDIUM GREEN PEPPER, CUT INTO 1 INCH PIECES
1 MEDIUM STALK CELERY, CHUNKED
1 SMALL ONION, CHOPPED
SALT AND PEPPER TO TASTE

## Cooking Instructions:

In a Dutch oven, brown the chicken pieces in oil until browned on all sides.
Add Chicken Concentrate mixture, and heat to boiling, then simmer for 2 hours.
Add vegetables and cook until tender, about 10 minutes.

# Chuck Wagon Stew

PREP TIME: 5 MINUTES
COOK TIME: 20 MINUTES
SERVES: 4

## Ingredient List:

1 POUND GROUND BEEF
2 MEDIUM POTATOES, CUT INTO 1/2 INCH CUBES
1/2 CUP GREEN ONION, MINCED
3 TABLESPOONS BEEF CONCENTRATE
1 CAN WHOLE TOMATOES (14.5 OUNCE)
1 CAN CUT GREEN BEANS (14.5 OUNCE)
SALT AND PEPPER TO TASTE

## Cooking Instructions:

In a deep skillet sauté ground beef until meat is light brown. Stir in potatoes, onion and Beef Concentrate, along with liquid from the canned tomatoes and beans. Heat to boiling, then reduce heat, cover and simmer for 15 minutes. Stir in tomatoes and beans. Break up tomatoes with a fork, cover and simmer until potatoes are cooked (about 6 minutes). Salt and pepper to taste.

# Egg Drop Soup

PREP TIME: 2 MINUTES
COOK TIME: 5 MINUTES
SERVES: 4

## Ingredient List:

3 TABLESPOONS CHICKEN CONCENTRATE MIXED WITH 1 QUART OF HOT WATER
1 CUP FROZEN PEAS
1 EGG, BEATEN
2 TABLESPOONS CHOPPED GREEN ONION FOR GARNISH — *optional*
SALT AND PEPPER TO TASTE

## Cooking Instructions:

In a medium saucepan, combine chicken stock and peas and heat to boiling. Drop egg into boiling soup; simmer uncover for 5 minutes. Remove from heat and garnish with green onions, if desired. Salt and pepper to taste.

# Quick and Easy Italian Stew

PREP TIME: 5 MINUTES
COOK TIME: 12 MINUTES
SERVES: 4

## Ingredient List:

3 1/2 TABLESPOONS OF BEEF CONCENTRATE MIXED WITH 8 TO 10 CUPS WATER

1 POUND ITALIAN SWEET SAUSAGE, CUT INTO 1/2 INCH SLICES

1 - 9 OUNCE BOX TORTELLINI PASTA

1 - 9 OUNCE BOX SPINACH TORTELLINI PASTA

1/2 POUND CABBAGE, SHREDDED

1 SMALL GREEN PEPPER, FINELY CHOPPED

1 MEDIUM ZUCCHINI, THINLY SLICED

1 SMALL RED ONION, FINELY CHOPPED

1 MEDIUM TOMATO, CHOPPED

1 TABLESPOON FRESH BASIL, CHOPPED

PARMESAN CHEESE, TO GRATE

SALT AND PEPPER TO TASTE

## Cooking Instructions:

In a large saucepot, combine all ingredients and bring to a boil over medium-high heat. Reduce heat and simmer until vegetables and pasta are tender, about 12 minutes. Serve with grated fresh Parmesan cheese. Salt and pepper to taste.

# TIP

*For a spicier stew, use Andouille or other hot sausage.*
*Even Kielbasa works beautifully in this stew.*

# Hot and Sour Soup

*You can't be a fan of Chinese food and not have a fondness for this classic soup. Unfortunately about the only time it's served at home is when it's delivered! But this tangy and healthy soup is so easy and quick that you can have it done faster yourself ...and without delivery charges!*

**PREP TIME: 10 MINUTES**
**COOK TIME: 15 MINUTES**
**SERVES: 8**

## Ingredient List:

4 CUPS WATER

4 TABLESPOONS CHICKEN CONCENTRATE

1/2 CUP COOKED SHREDDED PORK — *may substitute chicken*

1/4 CUP SOY SAUCE

2 TABLESPOONS WHITE VINEGAR

1 CUP DICED MUSHROOMS

1/2 CUP BAMBOO SHOOTS

1/2 TEASPOON MINCED FRESH GARLIC

1 1/2 TABLESPOONS SESAME OIL

1/8 TEASPOON CRUSHED RED PEPPER

2 TABLESPOONS CORNSTARCH, DISSOLVED IN 2 TABLESPOONS COLD WATER

2 EGGS, BEATEN

1/4 CUP THINLY SLICED GREEN ONIONS

## Cooking Instructions:

Add all the ingredients to a sauce pan (except the cornstarch, eggs and green onion) and bring to a simmer. Whisk in the dissolved cornstarch and continue simmering for about 4 minutes to thicken slightly.

Remove from heat, slowly add the beaten eggs and wait a few minutes for eggs to cook before serving with sliced green onion on top.

# TIP

*Leftovers like rotisserie chicken are perfect to substitute for the shredded pork in this recipe. To kick-up the flavor, try adding just a drop of sesame oil on top with the green onions before serving.*

# Chicken Tortilla Soup

PREP TIME: 10 MINUTES
COOK TIME: 10 MINUTES
SERVES: 4-6

## Ingredient List:

2/3 CUP CHOPPED ONION

3/4 TEASPOON GARLIC, MINCED

1/2 TABLESPOON VEGETABLE OIL

4 TABLESPOONS CHICKEN CONCENTRATE

1 CAN DICED TOMATOES (14.5 OUNCES)

1 TEASPOON DICED JALAPENO PEPPER

1/4 TEASPOON CHILI POWDER

1/8 TEASPOON GROUND CUMIN

1 POUND SKINLESS, BONELESS CHICKEN BREAST MEAT - CUBED

1/2 CUP FROZEN CORN

1/2 CUP CANNED BLACK BEANS

2 CUPS WATER

SALT AND PEPPER TO TASTE

2 TABLESPOONS AND 2 TEASPOONS SHREDDED MEXICAN CHEESE BLEND

2 TEASPOONS FRESH CILANTRO, MINCED

TORTILLA CHIPS

## Cooking Instructions:

In a large saucepan add onions, garlic and oil and lightly brown.
Add water, Chicken Concentrate, tomatoes, corn, black beans,
jalapeno pepper and spices. Reduce heat; cover and simmer for 4-6 minutes.
Add cubed chicken and cook until chicken is no longer pink.
Bring to a boil; cook and stir for 1 minute or until slightly thickened.
Top servings with cheese and cilantro.
Serve with tortilla chips if desired.

# BEEF

# Braised Short Ribs with
# Brussels Sprouts and Pearl Onions

*When it comes to Short Ribs, this is an unusual but delicious combination. These wine braised ribs braise slowly along with the brussels sprouts and pearl onions, each soaking up the sweetness of the wine. In a pressure cooker, they take on even more of the wine braised flavor.*

**PREP TIME: 15 MINUTES**
**COOK TIME: 1 HOUR IN PRESSURE COOKER, 3 HOURS IN THE OVEN.**
**SERVES: 4**

## Ingredient List:

2 TABLESPOONS VEGETABLE OIL

3-4 POUNDS SHORT RIBS, TRIMMED OF FAT — *seasoned with a pinch of salt & pepper*

1 ONION, HALVED THEN SLICED 1/4 INCH THICK

1 CUP DRY RED WINE

1 TEASPOON BEEF CONCENTRATE MIXED INTO 1 CUP WARM WATER

3 TABLESPOONS TOMATO PASTE

3 TABLESPOONS MINCED GARLIC

1 TEASPOON WORCESTERSHIRE SAUCE

12 BRUSSEL SPROUTS

1 CUP PEARL ONIONS

1 BAY LEAF

1 TEASPOON DRIED THYME

SALT AND PEPPER TO TASTE

## Cooking Instructions:

Add the vegetable oil to a pressure cooker set to brown or large Dutch oven over medium high heat. When oil is sizzling place short ribs and lightly brown on all sides. You will have to brown in at least two batches. Cover with the remaining ingredients and set pressure cooker and on high pressure for 60 minutes, or cover Dutch oven and put in 350 degree oven for 3 hours. When time is up, let pressure release naturally for 10 minutes from the pressure cooker. Remove lid and salt and pepper to taste. Serve over risotto, polenta, or mashed potatoes, or sweet potatoes.

# TIP
*This recipe is also great with an extremely dark beer in place of the red wine. Guinness is just about as dark as a beer gets!*

# Beef and Broccoli

PREP TIME: 5 MINUTES
COOK TIME: 10 MINUTES
SERVES: 4

## Ingredient List:

1 POUND BONELESS BEEF SIRLOIN STEAK OR BEEF TOP ROUND STEAK
1 TABLESPOON VEGETABLE OIL
2 TABLESPOONS BEEF CONCENTRATE ADDED TO 1 CUP WATER
3 TABLESPOONS SOY SAUCE
1 TABLESPOON RED WINE VINEGAR
1 TEASPOON GARLIC POWDER
1/4 TEASPOON CRUSHED RED PEPPER
3 CUPS BROCCOLI FLOWERETS, FRESH OR FROZEN
4 CUPS COOKED RICE, HEATED

## Cooking Instructions:

Slice beef into very thin strips. Heat oil in skillet. Add beef and stir-fry
until browned and juices evaporate. Add Concentrate water mixture, soy sauce,
vinegar, garlic powder and pepper. Heat to a boil.
Add broccoli and cook until tender-crisp. Serve over rice.

# Slow Cooked French Dip

PREP TIME: 5 MINUTES
COOK TIME: 7 HOURS
SERVES: 8-10

## Ingredient List:

4 POUNDS RUMP ROAST
2 TABLESPOONS BEEF CONCENTRATE ADDED TO 2 CUPS WATER
2 SLICED WHITE ONIONS
1 TEASPOON DRY THYME
6 FRENCH ROLLS

## Cooking Instructions:

Trim excess fat from the rump roast, and place in a slow cooker.
Add the Beef Concentrate, onion, thyme and water. Cook on low setting for 7 hours.
Preheat oven to 350 degrees. Split and warm French rolls.
Slice the meat thinly on the diagonal, and place on the rolls.
Serve the sauce for dipping.

# Fiesta Meatloaf

PREP TIME: 7-10 MINUTES
COOK TIME: 1 HOUR AND 30 MINUTES
SERVES: 6-8

## Ingredient List:

1 POUND LEAN GROUND BEEF

1 POUND LEAN GROUND PORK

3/4 CUP WARM WATER

2 SLIGHTLY BEATEN EGGS

1/3 CUP BLACK BEAN AND CORN SALSA

1 TABLESPOON GARLIC, CHOPPED

1/4 CUP GREEN ONION, DICED

3/4 CUP CRUSHED TORTILLA CHIPS

1/4 CUP GREEN BELL PEPPER, MINCED

2 TABLESPOONS BEEF CONCENTRATE

1/2 CUP SHREDDED MEXICAN CHEESE

## Cooking Instructions:

Preheat an oven to 350 degrees. Grease a 9x5 inch loaf pan.

Mix the beef, pork, water, Beef Concentrate, eggs, salsa, onion, crushed tortillas, garlic and bell pepper together in a mixing bowl until evenly blended.

Pack into the prepared loaf pan, poke holes into the loaf with a fork nearly to the bottom of the pan. Bake in the preheated oven until no longer pink in the center, about 1 1/2 hours. An instant-read thermometer inserted into the center should read 160 degrees.

Remove from oven and top with cheese before serving.

# Chicken Fried Steak

*This popular truck-stop comfort food has become an "Americana" mainstay. "Chicken Fried" refers to the fact that the steak is breaded and fried the same as chicken. And, it just so happens, the Southern White Gravy is great on fried chicken too! In fact, it's perfect poured on biscuits or even baked white fish; just add wine and lemon!*

**PREP TIME: 20 MINUTES**
**COOK TIME: 15 MINUTES**
**SERVES: 4**

## Ingredient List for Steak:

2-4 CUPS VEGETABLE OIL
2 EGGS, BEATEN
4 CUBE STEAKS; 4 OUNCES EACH — *may substitute any thinly sliced steak*

## Ingredient List for Seasoned Flour:

2 1/2 CUPS FLOUR
2 TEASPOONS SALT
1/2 TEASPOON BLACK PEPPER
1/2 TEASPOON GARLIC POWDER

## Ingredient List for Southern White Gravy:

2 1/2 CUPS MILK
2 TABLESPOONS CHICKEN CONCENTRATE
1/8 TEASPOON SALT
1/8 TEASPOON GARLIC POWDER
1/4 TEASPOON COARSE GROUND CRACKED BLACK PEPPER
2 TABLESPOONS BUTTER
2 TABLESPOONS FLOUR

## Cooking Instructions:

Fill a deep heavy pot with about 1 inch of oil, place over medium-high heat until temperature of oil reaches 350 degrees and maintain while oil is heating. Add the eggs to a small bowl and mix the seasoned flour ingredients in a larger bowl. Dip each steak into the flour, then egg and flour again and place into the pre-heated oil. Cook until golden brown on each side; about 3 to 4 minutes. Remove, drain on paper towels and keep warm. Place a sauce pan over medium-high heat, add all the Southern White Gravy ingredients, except the butter and flour, and bring to a slow simmer. While the milk heats, melt the butter in a small sauté pan over medium heat and whisk in the flour just until blended to make a roux*. Remove from heat and set aside. Once simmering, vigorously whisk in the roux* and continue stirring while cooking about 3 minutes more until sauce thickens. Remove from heat and smother the fried steaks to serve. Salt and pepper to taste and serve topped with sour cream.

# Beef Stroganoff

PREP TIME: 10 MINUTES
COOK TIME: 20-25 MINUTES
SERVES: 4-6

## Ingredient List:

1 POUND BEEF SIRLOIN STEAK, CUT INTO STRIPS

1/2 CUP CHOPPED ONION

1 TABLESPOON BUTTER

1/2 POUND SLICED FRESH MUSHROOMS

1/4 TEASPOON PEPPER

1/2 CUP WATER

1/2 CUP SOUR CREAM

2 TABLESPOONS BEEF CONCENTRATE

2 CUPS HOT COOKED EGG NOODLES

1 TABLESPOON CHOPPED FRESH PARSLEY

SALT AND PEPPER TO TASTE

## Cooking Instructions:

Cook meat and onions in large nonstick skillet on medium heat 5 to 6 minutes or until done. Remove from skillet; drain. Cover to keep warm. Add butter to skillet; cook until melted. Add mushrooms and pepper; cook 5 to 6 minutes or until mushrooms are tender.

Add water, Beef Concentrate and sour cream; cook and stir 2 minutes. Return meat to skillet; stir to combine ingredients. Cook 5 minutes. Remove from heat; let stand 5 minutes.

Salt and pepper to taste. Serve over hot noodles; sprinkle with parsley.

# Slowed Cooked Hungarian Goulash

*In traditional Hungarian cuisine, Goulashes were thick stews made by cattle herders or stockman from tough cuts of beef, seasoned with onions and most importantly Sweet Paprika, then slow cooked for hours to convert the tough collagen to gelatin, which along with the Paprika naturally thickens the stew. This Goulash is kicked up a notch with the addition of the Worcestershire sauce. If you wish, you may further thicken the Goulash at the end of cooking with a paste of flour and water.*

**PREP TIME: 10 MINUTES**
**COOK TIME: 9-10 HOURS**
**SERVES: 6-8**

## Ingredient List:

2 POUNDS BEEF CHUCK ROAST, CUBED

2 TABLESPOONS BEEF CONCENTRATE

1 LARGE ONION, DICED

1/2 CUP KETCHUP

2 TABLESPOONS WORCESTERSHIRE SAUCE

1 TABLESPOON BROWN SUGAR

2 TEASPOONS SALT

2 TEASPOONS HUNGARIAN SWEET PAPRIKA

1/2 TEASPOON DRY MUSTARD

1 1/4 CUPS WATER, DIVIDED

1 TEASPOON VEGETABLE CONCENTRATE

1/4 CUP ALL-PURPOSE FLOUR

SALT AND PEPPER TO TASTE

## Cooking Instructions:

Place beef in slow cooker, and cover with onion. In a medium bowl, stir together ketchup, Worcestershire sauce, brown sugar, salt, paprika, mustard, Vegetable and Beef Concentrates and 1 cup water. Pour mixture over beef and onions. Cover, and cook on low for 9 to 10 hours, or until meat is tender. Mix 1/4 cup water with flour to form a paste, and stir into Goulash. Cook on High for 10 to 15 minutes, or until sauce thickens. Salt and pepper to taste.

# TIP

*In Hungary, many Goulash recipes also call for the addition of caraway seeds to give it a distinctive flavor.*

# Savory Grilled Beef Kabobs

PREP TIME: 10 MINUTES + 30 MINUTES TO MARINATE
COOK TIME: 20 MINUTES
SERVES: 4

## Ingredient List:

2 TABLESPOONS BEEF CONCENTRATE ADDED TO 1 CUP WATER

1/2 CUP RED WINE

1/4 CUP DIJON MUSTARD

1/4 CUP KETCHUP

1 TABLESPOON VEGETABLE OIL

1 TEASPOON DRIED THYME LEAVES, CRUSHED

1/4 TEASPOON GARLIC, CHOPPED

1/2 TEASPOON GROUND BLACK PEPPER

1 BONELESS BEEF SIRLOIN STEAK, CUT INTO 1 TO 2 INCH CUBES

12 MEDIUM MUSHROOMS

1 LARGE GREEN PEPPER, CUT INTO 1-INCH PIECES

SALT AND PEPPER TO TASTE

## Cooking Instructions:

Add wine, Beef Concentrate mixture, ketchup, mustard, oil, thyme, garlic and black pepper in a shallow, nonmetallic dish or gallon size resealable plastic bag.
Add the beef, mushrooms and green pepper and toss to coat.
Cover the dish or seal the bag and refrigerate for 30 minutes.
Remove the beef and vegetables. Set the marinade aside.
Thread the beef, mushrooms and green pepper alternately on 4 skewers.
Lightly oil the grill rack and heat the grill to medium.
Grill the kabobs for 10-20 minutes or until the beef is cooked through and the vegetables are tender, turning and brushing often with the marinade.
Salt and pepper to taste.
Discard any remaining marinade.

# Steak Au Poivre

*The French version of pepper steak, Au Poivre, sounds like*
*an all-day affair in the kitchen and it usually is. But the steaks*
*cook in just 8 minutes and with this recipe now so does the sauce!*

**PREP TIME: 10 MINUTES**
**COOK TIME: 8 MINUTES**
**SERVES: 4**

## Ingredient List:

1 TABLESPOON OLIVE OIL

1 TABLESPOON BUTTER — *may substitute Olive or Canola oil*

4 SIRLOIN STEAKS (6 OUNCES EACH) — *may substitute Filet Mignon*

1/4 TEASPOON SALT

1/4 TEASPOON BLACK PEPPER

1 TABLESPOON RED ONION, MINCED

1/4 CUP BURGUNDY WINE — *may use substitute any red wine*

1 TEASPOON CHOPPED FRESH TARRAGON — *may use 1/4 teaspoon dry*

1/2 CUP HEAVY CREAM

1 TABLESPOON VEAL OR BEEF CONCENTRATE

1 TEASPOON CANNED GREEN PEPPERCORNS — *may use 1/2 teaspoon whole black peppercorns*

2 TABLESPOONS COLD WHOLE BUTTER — *optional*

## Cooking Instructions:

Place the oil and butter together in a large sauté pan over high heat until almost
smoking hot. Season the steaks with salt and pepper, add them to the hot pan
and sear for 2 minutes on each side. Add the onions, wine and tarragon and cook
for another 2 minutes to reduce. Stir cream and Concentrate into the pan and
continue cooking for about 2 minutes more or until sauce has reduced enough to
coat the back of a wooden spoon. Remove from heat, swirl in the cold butter
and serve garnished with fresh tarragon if desired.

# TIP

*Canned green peppercorns in brine are mild and may be found*
*in gourmet or ethnic food sections of grocery stores.*
*If not simply use cracked black pepper*
*or a few whole peppercorns as an alternative.*

# Grilled Stuffed Burgers

PREP TIME: 5 MINUTES
COOK TIME: 10-20 MINUTES
SERVES: 4-8

## Ingredient List:

2 POUNDS LEAN GROUND BEEF

1 TABLESPOON BEEF CONCENTRATE

1 TABLESPOON WORCESTERSHIRE SAUCE

1/2 CUP BLUE CHEESE, CRUMBLED

3/4 CUP ONION, CHOPPED

## Cooking Instructions:

Preheat an outdoor grill for medium high heat and lightly oil grate.
In a large bowl, combine the beef, onion, blue cheese, Beef Concentrate
and Worcestershire sauce. Mix together well and form into patties.
Grill patties over medium high heat for 10 to 20 minutes,
or to desired doneness.

# Simple Roast Beef Au Jus

*Sometimes the simplest food and preparation can provide amazing results and it just doesn't get easier or more satisfying than this slow roasted thinly sliced rare beef swimming in Au Jus. Simple goodness, simply done, simply delicious!*

**PREP TIME: 10 MINUTES**
**COOK TIME: 4+ HOURS**
**SERVES: 8-10**

## Ingredient List:

4 POUNDS BONELESS SIRLOIN TIP ROAST — *may use Prime Rib or similar*

1 1/2 TEASPOONS BLACK PEPPER

1/2 TEASPOON MINCED FRESH GARLIC

1/2 CUP KOSHER SALT

## Aus Jus Ingredient List:

4 CUPS WATER

3 TABLESPOONS BEEF CONCENTRATE

2 LARGE BAY LEAVES

1/4 TEASPOON SALT

1/4 TEASPOON BLACK PEPPER

## Cooking Instructions:

Preheat the oven to 225 degrees.

Place the roast in a shallow roasting pan, fat side up.

Season with salt, pepper, and garlic. Layer top of roast completely with the kosher salt.

Bake uncovered for about 4 hours or until a meat thermometer inserted into the thickest part of the roast registers 140 to 145 degrees (for rare).

Scrape off and discard the salt cap and let the meat rest for before thinly slicing.

Meanwhile to make the Au Jus, add all the Au Jus ingredients to a deep sauce pan over medium-high heat and bring to a simmer for 4 minutes.

Serve hot over the sliced roast beef or on the side in a cup for dipping.

# TIP

*When roast beef Au Jus is served hot as a dinner
it is commonly referred to as London broil and when served
on a roll with a cup of hot Au Jus on the side
it's the classic French Dip sandwich.*

# Italian Baked Meatballs

**PREP TIME: 15 MINUTES**
**COOK TIME: 1 HOUR 30 MINUTES**
**SERVES: 8-12**

## Ingredient List:

3 POUND PACKAGE OF GROUND BEEF, VEAL OR PORK

1 YELLOW ONION, DICED

4 EGGS, BEATEN

2 CUPS PLAIN BREADCRUMBS

1/2 CUP GRATED PARMESAN OR PECORINO CHEESE

1/2 CUP WARM WATER

2 TABLESPOONS BEEF CONCENTRATE

1/2 TEASPOON FRESHLY GROUND PEPPER

1 TABLESPOON OREGANO

1/4 CUP FRESH PARSLEY LEAVES, CHOPPED

1/2 TEASPOON DRIED BASIL

## Cooking Instructions:

Mix Beef Concentrate into the 1/2 cup of warm water.
In a large bowl combine all ingredients.
Mix thoroughly; making sure ingredients are evenly combined.
Using a tablespoon, scoop and shape the meat mixture into golf ball size
meatballs. Place meatballs in baking dish.
Preheat oven to 350 degrees.
Place baking disk in the preheated oven for 1 hour or until meatballs
are browned and cooked through. Add to your favorite spaghetti sauce.
Heat and simmer, allowing the meatballs to flavor the sauce.

# Sirloin Chili Supreme

*Supreme is a term traditionally used to signify a version
of a recipe that is richer in flavor. Either by adding cream, butter
or in this instance, an abundance of natural flavors and seasonings
all enriched further by the flavor-packed Veal or Beef Concentrate!*

**PREP TIME: 20 MINUTES**
**COOK TIME: 15 MINUTES**
**SERVES: 8**

## Ingredient List:

2 TABLESPOONS OLIVE OIL

2 POUNDS GROUND SIRLOIN

1 LARGE RED BELL PEPPER, CHOPPED

1 LARGE GREEN BELL PEPPER, CHOPPED

1/2 CUP RED ONION, CHOPPED

1 TABLESPOON VEAL OR BEEF CONCENTRATE

1/4 CUP CHILI POWDER

1/4 CUP CUMIN

2 TEASPOONS SALT

1 TEASPOON FRESH GARLIC, MINCED

1/2 TEASPOON BLACK PEPPER

1/4 TEASPOON GARLIC POWDER

1/4 TEASPOON CAYENNE PEPPER

1 CAN DICED TOMATOES (14-16 OUNCES)

1 CAN TOMATO SAUCE (8 OUNCES)

1 CAN BLACK BEANS, DRAINED AND RINSED (15 OUNCE)

## Cooking Instructions:

Heat the oil in a large deep skillet over medium-high heat. Add the ground sirloin
and cook until browned. Drain any excess fat, add the peppers and onions and cook
just until tender. Stir in all remaining ingredients and simmer for 10 minutes while
stirring occasionally. Serve garnished with sour cream and fresh cilantro if desired.

## TIP
*Any variety of ground beef may be used in place of the ground sirloin.
And make it decadent by topping with melted shredded
cheddar jack cheese and fresh diced onions.*

# POULTRY

# Stuffed Chicken and Spinach Cannelloni

PREP TIME: 20 MINUTES
COOK TIME: 45 MINUTES
SERVES: 4

## Ingredient List:

8 CANNELLONI NOODLES
4 CLOVES GARLIC, MINCED
4 SHALLOTS, CHOPPED
2 TABLESPOONS OLIVE OIL
1/2 CUP DRY SHERRY
1 8OZ PACKAGE CREAM CHEESE
1/2 CUP RICOTTA CHEESE
SALT AND PEPPER TO TASTE
1/2 ONION, CHOPPED
1/4 CUP SUNDRIED TOMATOES
1 CUP OF COOKED GRILLED CHICKEN, DICED
2 TABLESPOONS CHICKEN CONCENTRATE
1 TEASPOON FRESH BASIL, DICED
2 CUPS OF FRESH SPINACH
2 CUPS HEAVY CREAM
1 CUP GRATED PARMESAN CHEESE

## Cooking Instructions:

In a large pot of salted water, parboil cannelloni (parboiling is partially cooking
the noodles in boiling water; they will finish cooking when baked).
Meanwhile, cook 1/2 of minced garlic and 1/2 of chopped shallots in
1 tablespoon olive oil in a medium saucepan over medium heat for 30 seconds.
Pour in sherry, raise heat to high and reduce liquid by half. Stir in cream and
1/2 cup of Parmesan cheese. Reduce until there is about 2 cups liquid.
Remove from heat, and season with salt and pepper to taste. Set cream sauce
aside to cool. In a large skillet, heat one tablespoon olive oil over medium heat.
Cook onion, add remaining shallots and garlic and cook until lightly browned.
Add Chicken Concentrate, spinach and sundried tomatoes. Cook for only
1 minute. Transfer to a large bowl. Stir in diced chicken, fresh basil, ricotta
cheese, cream cheese and 1/2 cup of Parmesan cheese. Season to taste with salt
and pepper. Set filling aside. Preheat oven to 350 degrees. Lightly grease one
9x13 inch baking dish. Stuff cheese filling into cannelloni. Place in prepared
baking dish, and cover with cream sauce. Bake in preheated oven for 25 minutes.

# Chicken Amaretto

*Floribbean cuisine was born in the mid 80's out of a mixture of California cuisine with Caribbean influences like tropical fruits in the kitchens of south Florida. This delightful "Floribbean" chicken dish takes you straight to the Caribbean; by way of Miami, that is!*

**PREP TIME: 15 MINUTES**
**COOK TIME: 10 MINUTES**
**SERVES: 4**

## Ingredient List:

1 TABLESPOON OLIVE OIL

1 TABLESPOON BUTTER — *may substitute any oil*

4-4 OUNCE CHICKEN BREAST CUTLETS

1/4 TEASPOON SALT

1/4 TEASPOON BLACK PEPPER

1/4 CUP FLOUR, FOR DUSTING CHICKEN

1/2 CUP HEAVY CREAM

1 TEASPOON CHICKEN CONCENTRATE

1 OUNCE AMARETTO LIQUOR — *may substitute 2 drops of Almond Extract*

2 TABLESPOONS DRY COCONUT FLAKES

2 TABLESPOONS SLICED ALMONDS, TOASTED

## Cooking Instructions:

Add the oil and butter to a large sauté pan over high heat, until sizzling.
Season the chicken with salt and pepper, dust lightly in flour and add to the pan.
Cook until golden brown, about 2 minutes each side.
Add heavy cream, Chicken Concentrate and Amaretto and swirl
the pan while cooking 2 minutes more or until sauce thickens.
Serve each cutlet topped with coconut flakes and toasted almonds.

# TIP

*You can make this same recipe with white fish
such as filet of sole, tilapia or even mahi.*
*enjoy!*

# Chicken and Sausage Gumbo

*Gumbo originated in Southern Louisiana during the 18th century. It is a thick stew which always contains the holy trinity of celery, bell peppers and onions. Sometimes made with fish alone, but more often it contains chicken and sausage.*

**PREP TIME: 10 MINUTES**
**COOK TIME: 2 HOURS AND 30 MINUTES**
**SERVES: 6-8**

## Ingredient List:

1 CUP VEGETABLE OIL

1 CUP ALL-PURPOSE FLOUR

1 LARGE ONION, CHOPPED

1 LARGE GREEN BELL PEPPER, CHOPPED

2 CELERY STALKS, CHOPPED

1 POUND ANDOUILLE SAUSAGE

4 CLOVES GARLIC, MINCED

SALT AND PEPPER TO TASTE

CREOLE SEASONING TO TASTE

6 CUPS WATER

6 TABLESPOONS CHICKEN CONCENTRATE

1 BAY LEAF

1 ROTISSERIE CHICKEN, BONED AND SHREDDED

## Cooking Instructions:

Heat the oil in a Dutch oven over medium heat.
Add onions, celery and green peppers. When hot, whisk in flour.
Continue whisking until the roux* resembles the color of chocolate milk, 8 to 10 minutes. Do not burn. Add sausage into the roux; cook 5 minutes.
Stir in the garlic and cook another 5 minutes.
Season with salt, pepper, and Creole seasoning; blend thoroughly.
Pour in the water and Chicken Concentrate and add the bay leaf.
Bring to a boil over high heat, and then reduce heat to medium-low, and simmer uncovered, for 1 hour, stirring occasionally.
Stir in the chicken, and simmer 1 hour more.
Skim off any foam that floats to the top during the last hour.
Eat with white rice if desired.

# Tarragon Chicken

*Believed to have been brought to Europe from Mongolia, Tarragon quickly became popular especially for its affinity to chicken.*

PREP TIME: 10 MINUTES
COOK TIME: 30-35 MINUTES
SERVES: 4

## Ingredient List:

4 BONELESS, SKINLESS CHICKEN BREAST HALVES

1/2 TEASPOON PAPRIKA

1/3 CUP BUTTER, DIVIDED

2 TABLESPOONS FLOUR

2 MEDIUM ZUCCHINI, JULIENNED*

4 SMALL CARROTS, JULIENNED*

4 LARGE MUSHROOMS, SLICED

2 TABLESPOON MINCED FRESH TARRAGON

2 TABLESPOON CHICKEN CONCENTRATE

1/4 CUP WHITE WINE

1/2 TEASPOON SALT

1/8 TEASPOON PEPPER

ONE 1 GALLON RESEALABLE PLASTIC BAG

## Cooking Instructions:

Blend paprika and flour in a resealable plastic bag.

Add chicken into bag and coat well.

In a large skillet, brown chicken in 2 teaspoons butter.

Place the vegetables in a greased 13x9x2 inch baking dish.

Top the vegetables with flour and paprika coated chicken.

Melt the remaining butter; stir in the tarragon, Chicken Concentrate, white wine, salt and pepper. Pour over chicken and vegetables.

Cover and bake at 350 degrees for 30-35 minutes or until chicken juices run clear and vegetables are tender.

# Teriyaki Chicken

PREP TIME: 5 MINUTES + 3 HOURS TO MARINATE
COOK TIME: 1 HOUR
SERVES: 4

## Ingredient List:

1 WHOLE CHICKEN, CUT IN PIECES (3 POUNDS)

3/4 CUP GRANULATED SUGAR

2 TABLESPOONS CHICKEN CONCENTRATE

3/4 CUP SOY SAUCE

1 TABLESPOON GRATED FRESH GINGER

2 CLOVES GARLIC, MINCED

4 GREEN ONIONS, CHOPPED FOR GARNISH — *optional*

## Cooking Instructions:

Rinse chicken pieces, and pat dry with paper towels.

Place chicken cut side down in a 9x13 inch baking dish.

In a medium mixing bowl, combine sugar, Chicken Concentrate, soy sauce, grated ginger and garlic. Mix well, and pour mixture over chicken.

Cover and refrigerate for at least 3 hours.

Preheat oven to 350 degrees.

Bake chicken uncovered in the preheated oven for 1 hour, basting frequently with marinade.

Test for doneness, making sure there is no pink left inside (165 degrees).

Let cool slightly, then cut into smaller pieces.

Top with chopped green onion and serve.

# Grilled Herb Chicken

**PREP TIME: 5 MINUTES + 2 HOURS TO MARINATE**
**COOK TIME: 12-14 MINUTES**
**SERVES: 4-6**

## Ingredient List:

1 TABLESPOON AND 1 TEASPOON ITALIAN FLAT LEAF PARSLEY, CHOPPED

1-1/4 TEASPOONS FRESH ROSEMARY, MINCED

1-1/4 TEASPOONS FRESH THYME, CHOPPED

3/4 TEASPOON DRIED SAGE

2 CLOVES GARLIC, MINCED

3 TABLESPOONS CHICKEN CONCENTRATE

2 TABLESPOONS AND 2 TEASPOONS OLIVE OIL

1/3 CUP BALSAMIC VINEGAR

SALT AND PEPPER TO TASTE

1 POUND SKINLESS, BONELESS CHICKEN BREASTS

ONE 1 GALLON RESEALABLE PLASTIC BAG

## Cooking Instructions:

In a blender combine the parsley, rosemary, thyme, sage, garlic, Chicken
Concentrate, oil, vinegar, salt and pepper to taste. Blend together.
Place chicken in resealable plastic bag and pour blended marinade over the chicken.
Zip closed and refrigerate to marinate for at least 2 hours.
Preheat grill to medium high heat.
Remove chicken from bag; (disposing of leftover marinade) and grill for about
6 to 7 minutes per side, or until chicken is cooked through and no longer
pink inside(165 degrees). Use the grilled chicken on top a salad or make chicken
salad. Place on a bun for a juicy sandwich with lettuce and tomato or even
dice the chicken and add to a soup!

# Slowed Cooked Tuscan Chicken

*This is an everyday way of cooking chicken in Tuscany using typical Italian herbs and cheese.*

**PREP TIME: 10 MINUTES**
**COOK TIME: 6-8 HOURS**
**SERVES: 4**

## Ingredient List:

1 WHOLE CHICKEN CUT INTO PIECES

1 (4.5 OUNCE) CAN CHOPPED RIPE OLIVES, DRAINED

2 TABLESPOONS OLIVE OR VEGETABLE OIL, DIVIDED

1/2 TEASPOON DRIED OREGANO

2 TABLESPOONS RED WINE

1 CAN OF DICED TOMATOES (14.5 OUNCES)

2 CUPS OF WATER

3 TABLESPOONS CHICKEN CONCENTRATE

1 TEASPOON SUGAR

1 TEASPOON BALSAMIC VINEGAR

1 GARLIC CLOVE, MINCED

1/4 TEASPOON DRIED THYME

1 MEDIUM ONION, SLICED

1/2 CUP OF GRATED ITALIAN CHEESE — *may use Romano, Asiago or Parmesan*

## Cooking Instructions:

Add ingredients (except chicken) to a large crock pot and mix thoroughly.
Add chicken pieces.
Cook on medium heat for 6 hours.
Plate chicken and smother in sauce from crock pot.
Top with grated cheese.
Serve with rice, roasted potatoes or a side of pasta.

# Chicken Marsala

*If you have ever attended a family reunion or banquet
then most likely you have enjoyed this classic comfort food
of Chicken smothered in brown sauce and wine.
Especially popular with caterers, now you too can cook like
the pros for your next gathering or for dinner anytime!*

**PREP TIME: 10 MINUTES**
**COOK TIME: 6 MINUTES**
**SERVES: 4**

### Ingredient List:

2 TABLESPOONS OLIVE OIL

4-4 OUNCE CHICKEN BREAST CUTLETS

1/4 TEASPOON SALT

1/4 TEASPOON BLACK PEPPER

1/4 CUP FLOUR, FOR DUSTING CHICKEN

1/2 CUP SLICED BUTTON MUSHROOMS

1 TABLESPOON MINCED RED ONION

1/4 CUP MARSALA WINE

1/2 CUP HEAVY CREAM

1 TABLESPOON VEAL OR BEEF CONCENTRATE

1/2 TEASPOON FRESH CHOPPED PARSLEY FOR GARNISH — *optional*

### Cooking Instructions:

Add the oil to a large sauté pan over high heat until sizzling.
Season the chicken with salt and pepper, dust lightly in flour and add to the pan.
Cook about 2 minutes until golden brown, flip over and add the mushrooms
and onions and cook for 2 more minutes. Pour in the Marsala to sizzle, stir cream
and Concentrate into the pan and continue cooking for about 2 minutes more
or until sauce lightly coats the back of a wooden spoon.
Serve sprinkled with chopped parsley if desired.

## TIP

*This is a great meal for feeding the masses!
Simply make the chicken and sauce separately ahead of time and
combine in roasting pans and heat in the oven when you're ready to serve!*

# PORK

*A pulled pork sandwich may seem like such a simple picnic indulgence,
but preparing one the traditional way will take about 8 hours.
You can use this recipe to cook the pork for 8 hours in the oven or
smoker or you can take the short cut of using a pressure cooker.*

**PREP TIME: 11 MINUTES**
**COOK TIME: 90 MINUTES IN PRESSURE COOKER OR 8 HOURS IN A SMOKER OR DUTCH OVEN**
**SERVES: 10**

## Ingredient List for Dry Rub:

1 TABLESPOON CHILI POWDER

2 TEASPOONS GROUND CUMIN

1/4 TEASPOON GROUND ALLSPICE

2 TEASPOONS SALT

1 TEASPOON GROUND BLACK PEPPER

## Ingredient List for Pulled Pork:

4-5 POUND PORK SHOULDER OR BUTT

1 TEASPOON CHICKEN CONCENTRATE MIXED WITH 1 CUP HOT WATER

1 TEASPOON LIQUID SMOKE

2 CUPS OF YOUR FAVORITE BBQ SAUCE

## Suggested Options:

YOUR FAVORITE VARIETY OF BUN

SLICED RED ONION

CHEDDAR CHEESE SLICES

## Cooking Instructions:

Preheat the oven to 325 degrees. Combine all Dry Rub ingredients in a small
bowl. Cut pork into 2 inch thick pieces (to speed up cooking time) then cut 1/8
inch deep, crisscrossing grooves into the pieces. Coat pieces with Dry Rub,
pushing it into the grooves. Let sit or five minutes. Add the Chicken Concentrate
in the hot water and liquid smoke to a pressure cooker or Dutch oven.
Pour BBQ Sauce over pork pieces and securely lock the pressure cooker's lid or
cover the Dutch oven. Set the pressure cooker to high and cook for 90 minutes or
if using a Dutch oven, place in oven for eight hours. If using a pressure cooker, let
pressure release naturally for at least 10 minutes, before quick releasing any
remaining pressure and safely removing lid. If using a Dutch oven or smoker,
remove from oven. Pork should be fork tender and shred easily. Serve pulled apart
on buns with your favorite toppings such as red onion and cheddar cheese.

# Pork Pot Roast

*This classic family meal is like two recipes in one.*
*The first is the pot roast dinner and the second is the sliced pork*
*or Cuban sandwich made from the leftovers the next day!*

**PREP TIME: 15 MINUTES**
**COOK TIME: 2 AND 1/2 HOURS**
**SERVES: 6**

## Ingredient List for Roast:

4 TABLESPOONS VEGETABLE OIL
2-3 POUND PORK LOIN, SHOULDER OR BUTT — *seasoned with 1/2 teaspoon of salt & pepp*
1/2 CUP DRY WHITE WINE
2 TEASPOONS CHICKEN CONCENTRATE MIXED INTO 2 CUPS HOT WATER
2 TABLESPOONS GARLIC, MINCED
1 SPRIG FRESH THYME — *may use 1 teaspoon dried*
2 BAY LEAVES

## Ingredient List for Vegetables:

6 SMALL RED SKIN POTATOES, HALVED
2 SMALL ONIONS, PEELED AND QUARTERED
1 CUP BABY CARROTS
2 STALKS CELERY, CUT INTO 1 INCH PIECES
2 TABLESPOONS CORNSTARCH
SALT AND PEPPER TO TASTE

## Cooking Instructions:

Add the vegetable oil to a roasting pan or Dutch oven and set over medium high heat.
Add the seasoned pot roast and brown well on all sides, about six minutes.
Add the remaining "Roast" ingredients, reserving the vegetables, place in preheated
oven for 2 hours. Add vegetables to the roasting pan and cook for another half hour or
until vegetables are tender. Remove the roast and vegetables, and set aside to rest under
tin foil as you thicken the gravy. To thicken gravy: set the pan on the stove over medium
high heat. Mix cornstarch with 2 tablespoons water and slowly add to simmering juice,
stirring constantly, until thick. Carve roast and serve with vegetables and gravy.

# TIP

*This recipe, without the vegetables is a must for a good homemade Cuban*
*sandwich with sliced pork, ham, Swiss cheese, pickles and mustard.*
*Sliced pork lunchmeat is hard to come by in grocery stores —*
*its texture usually bears more resemblance to bologna than pork.*

# Pork Loin Chops with Apple & Sherry

*It's no secret that pork and apple are meant to be together. In this recipe the juicy, boneless pork loin chops cook surrounded by thick cut apples, sherry, cinnamon and a little touch of brown sugar for a sweet note that's delicious but not overwhelming. Serve this in the fall when apples are at their peak.*

**PREP TIME: 15 MINUTES**
**COOK TIME: 35 MINUTES**
**SERVES: 4**

## Ingredient List:

2 TABLESPOONS CANOLA OIL

4 PORK LOIN CHOPS, 1 INCH THICK CENTER-CUT

1/2 RED ONION, DICED

2 LARGE APPLES, PEELED, CORED AND CUT INTO 8 WEDGES EACH

1/2 CUP DRY SHERRY

1/2 TEASPOON CHICKEN CONCENTRATE MIXED WITH 1/2 CUP HOT WATER

1/2 TEASPOON VEGETABLE CONCENTRATE MIXED WITH 1/2 CUP HOT WATER

2 TABLESPOONS BUTTER

1 TABLESPOON BROWN SUGAR

1/2 TEASPOON CINNAMON

SALT AND PEPPER TO TASTE

## Cooking Instructions:

Preheat the oven to 325 degrees.

Add the oil to a large skillet or Dutch oven, set over medium to high heat until almost smoking. Season the pork chops with salt and pepper.

Place in the hot skillet or Dutch oven and sear for 2 to 4 minutes on each side until crispy brown. Reduce heat to medium and add diced onion and simmer until soft. In a mixing bowl stir together remaining ingredients, then add to hot pan. Cover the pan and cook in oven for 35 minutes.

Serve chops drizzled with cooking liquid.

# TIP

*Any cut of pork chop will work well in this recipe, boneless or bone-in.*
*You can even save money by buying the entire pork loin and*
*cutting the chops off yourself, freezing the rest of the loin for future meals.*

# Pork Loin with Milk Gravy

*While the idea of simmering a pork loin in milk may sound strange,
it really highlights the wonderful flavors of the meat itself. In fact, the flavors it
brings out are so wonderful that a tiny pinch of rosemary is the only herb in the dish.*

PREP TIME: 10 MINUTES
COOK TIME: 2 HOURS
SERVES: 6

## Ingredient List:

2 TABLESPOONS BUTTER

1 TABLESPOON VEGETABLE OIL

2-3 POUND PORK LOIN

1 TABLESPOON MINCED GARLIC

1 CUP DRY WHITE WINE

1 TEASPOON CHICKEN CONCENTRATE MIXED WITH 1 CUP OF HOT WATER

1/4 TEASPOON DRIED ROSEMARY

1 CUP WHOLE MILK

2 TABLESPOONS CORNSTARCH

SALT AND PEPPER TO TASTE

## Cooking Instructions:

Preheat oven to 350 degrees.

Add the butter, oil and pork loin to a Dutch oven and over medium high heat.
Brown with lid off until loin is lightly browned on all side, about six minutes.
Stir together remaining ingredients (except for the cornstarch) in a mixing bowl and
add to the Dutch oven. Place in oven and cook for 1 hour and 50 minutes.
Remove from oven and place Dutch oven over medium heat on the stove.
Add milk and simmer for 10 minutes. Remove roast to rest under tin foil as you
thicken the gravy. To thicken gravy: mix cornstarch with 2 tablespoons water and
slowly add to simmering juices, stirring constantly, until thick.
Salt and pepper gravy to taste.

# TIP

*To give the gravy an extra tang:
add 1/4 teaspoon chicken concentrate into the cornstarch slurry\*.*

# Two Can Cola Pork Roast

*This spectacular pork roast recipe is by far the greatest mystery in this book. Just how cola make gravy that is this good? The answer is not known ...but it certainly is delicious and definitely not as sweet as you would think it to be.*

**PREP TIME: 20 MINUTES**
**COOK TIME: 2+ HOURS**
**SERVES: 6**

## Ingredient List:

2 TABLESPOONS CANOLA OIL

2-3 POUND PORK LOIN, SHOULDER OR BUTT

2 CANS REGULAR COLA — *you know... the one in the red can!*

1 PACKET POWDERED ONION SOUP MIX

1 TEASPOON VEGETABLE CONCENTRATE

2 TABLESPOONS CORNSTARCH

SALT AND PEPPER TO TASTE

## Cooking Instructions:

Preheat the oven to 325 degrees.
Add the oil to a large skillet or Dutch oven, set over medium to high heat until the oil is almost smoking. Season the roast with salt, pepper, and garlic. Place in the hot skillet or Dutch oven and sear for 2 to 4 minutes on each side until crispy brown.
In a mixing bowl whisk together the onion soup mix and the cola.
Add the mixture to the pan with the browned roast, cover, and bake for 2 hours or until meat is fork tender.
Remove roast to rest under tin foil while making the gravy.
To thicken gravy: set the roasting vessel on the stove at medium high.
Whisk the cornstarch with 2 tablespoons of water to make a slurry*.
Slowly add to simmering pan juices, stirring constantly, until thick.
Serve roast sliced smothered in the pan gravy. A tablespoon of cold butter may be added to the gravy for richness if desired.

# TIP
*Try a pork roast with mashed potatoes and fresh green beans!*

# Baby Back Ribs

*Nothing says comfort quite like this flavorful dish!*
*The combination of tangy barbecue sauce and tender meat will satisfy*
*the heartiest of appetites. Pair them with coleslaw & corn on the cob ...you'll*
*have a picnic lunch. Pair them with mashed potatoes & green beans ...you*
*have a full-fledge country supper!*

**PREP TIME: 10 MINUTES**
**COOK TIME: 1 HOUR**
**SERVES: 6**

### Ingredient List:

1/2 CUP WATER

1 TEASPOON VEGETABLE CONCENTRATE

3 POUNDS BABY BACK PORK RIBS

2 CUPS OF YOUR FAVORITE BBQ SAUCE

### Cooking Instructions:

Preheat oven to 350 degrees.
Combine water and concentrate to bottom of Dutch oven or roasting pan.
Cut ribs into sections small enough to fit your pan and generously coat with
the BBQ sauce. Lean ribs against sides of pans, standing upright in the pan.
Add any remaining BBQ sauce to water in the bottom of the pan, and cover.
Place ribs in preheated oven for 1 hour.

# TIP

*To give the ribs a little more color and flavor, place cooked ribs*
*on a sheet pan under the broiler for a few minutes*
*until the sugars in the sauce begin to char.*

# VEAL
# & LAMB

# Roast Rack of Lamb with Roasted Vegetables

*Rack of Lamb is increasingly available in most grocery stores with the bones already scraped, and the meat trimmed of excess fat. All you really need to do is season and brown the rack in a skilled, then throw the rack into the oven. Serve these with roasted vegetables that have had their flavor enhanced with a teaspoon of Vegetable Concentrate.*

**PREP TIME: 15 MINUTES**
**COOK TIME: 30 MINUTES**
**SERVES: 2**

## Roast Rack of Lamb Ingredient List:

1 TABLESPOON EXTRA VIRGIN OLIVE OIL
1 PRE-TRIMMED RACK OF LAMB (1 TO 2 POUNDS)
1 TEASPOON SALT
1/2 TEASPOON GROUND BLACK PEPPER
1/4 TEASPOON GARLIC POWDER
4 SPRIGS FRESH MINT FOR GARNISH — *optional*

## Roasted Vegetables Ingredient List:

1/4 CUP OLIVE OIL
3 RIBS CELERY, CUT INTO THIRDS
2 MEDIUM YELLOW SQUASH, HALVED CROSSWISE
2 MEDIUM ZUCCHINI, HALVED CROSSWISE
1 MEDIUM YELLOW ONION, QUARTERED
1 RED BELL PEPPER, CORED, SEEDED AND QUARTERED
1 CLOVE GARLIC, MINCED
1 1/2 TEASPOONS KOSHER SALT
1 TEASPOON DRIED OREGANO
1 TEASPOON PAPRIKA
1/4 TEASPOON GROUND BLACK PEPPER
1/8 TEASPOON GARLIC POWDER
1 TEASPOON OF VEGETABLE CONCENTRATE

## Cooking Instructions for Rack of Lamb:

Preheat the oven to 450 degrees. Place the oil in a sauté pan over high heat until almost smoking. Season both sides of the rack of lamb with the salt, pepper and garlic powder. Place whole rack, meaty side down, in the hot pan. Brown for about 3 to 5 minutes (on meaty side only) until meat is well seared. Place the lamb rack, seared side up, on a small sheet pan or roasting pan and bake in the oven until a meat thermometer (stuck into the thickest part of the lamb) reads 140 degrees for rare, about 30 minutes.
Let rest for about 5 minutes and then slice in between each bone to make individual chops and serve garnished with fresh mint if desired.

## Cooking Instructions for Roasted Vegetables:

Toss all of the ingredients in a large bowl thoroughly coating with the seasonings, oil and Concentrate. Arrange vegetables in the roasting pan to leave space between each piece. Roast along with the lamb for about 30 to 40 minutes or until the lamb is done.

# Braised Lamb Shanks with Lemon and Mint

*Even if you hail from the heart of Scandinavia, you'll be saying "Opa!"
when you taste this delicious, traditional Greek pairing of flavors.
The sharpness of the lemon and the fresh taste of the mint are perfect
compliments to the unique flavor of the lamb.*

**PREP TIME: 15 MINUTES**
**COOK TIME: 45 MINUTES IN PRESSURE COOKER, 2 HOURS IN THE OVEN**
**SERVES: 6**

## Ingredient List:

2 TABLESPOONS VEGETABLE OIL
3 LAMB SHANKS, CUT IN HALF, EXCESS FAT TRIMMED OFF
1 TABLESPOON GARLIC, MINCED
1 CUP DRY WHITE WINE
2 TEASPOONS CHICKEN CONCENTRATE MIXED INTO 2 CUPS OF WARM WATER
3 TABLESPOONS TOMATO PASTE
1 LEMON, SLICED THICK
1 TABLESPOON FRESH MINT, CHOPPED
1 ONION, SLICED THICK
2 CARROTS, CUT INTO 2 INCH LENGTHS
2 STALKS CELERY, CUT INTO 2 INCH LENGTHS
SALT AND PEPPER TO TASTE
ZEST OF 1 LEMON — *to top*
FRESH MINT, CHOPPED — *to top*

## Cooking Instructions:

Heat the oil in a pressure cooker on brown or in a Dutch oven on the stovetop on
medium high heat. Add the lamb shanks and brown well on all sides.
When almost browned, add garlic to infuse it into the meat. Add wine, Chicken
Concentrate mixed with water, tomato paste, sliced lemon and fresh mint and
in pressure cooker lock the lid, and cook on high pressure for 40 minutes.
In the Dutch oven cover and cook in preheated 300 degree oven for 2 hours or until
shanks are tender. When done, remove lid from pressure cooker or Dutch oven add
onion, carrots and celery. Cook in pressure cooker for an additional 5 minutes at
high pressure or in the Dutch oven for an additional 15 minutes. In the pressure
cooker, let the pressure release naturally. Remove lids from cooker or Dutch oven.
Salt and pepper to taste. Serve topped with lemon zest and fresh chopped mint.

# TIP

*Lamb shoulder can also be used in place of the shanks
by having your butcher cut the shoulder into 2 inch pieces.*

# Veal Francaise

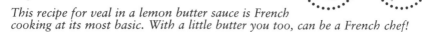

*This recipe for veal in a lemon butter sauce is French cooking at its most basic. With a little butter you too, can be a French chef!*

PREP TIME: 15 MINUTES
COOK TIME: 6 MINUTES IN THE PRESSURE COOKER, 20 MINUTES ON THE STOVETOP
SERVES: 4

## Ingredient List:

1-2 POUNDS VEAL SCALLOPINI (ABOUT 1/2 INCH THICK)

1 CUP FLOUR, MIXED WITH PINCH OF SALT AND PEPPER

1 TABLESPOON OLIVE OIL

3 TABLESPOONS BUTTER OR MARGARINE

1 TABLESPOON GARLIC, MINCED

1/2 TEASPOON VEAL OR CHICKEN CONCENTRATE MIXED INTO 1/2 CUP WARM WATER

1/2 CUP DRY WHITE WINE

1/2 CUP LEMON JUICE

1 TABLESPOON CORNSTARCH — *optional*

SALT AND PEPPER TO TASTE

1 LEMON, SLICED THIN, FOR GARNISH — *optional*

## Cooking Instructions:

Dip veal scallopini in seasoned flour until they are well coated.
Pour the olive oil and butter into a pressure cooker set on high or brown.
Or use a large heavy skillet, set to medium high heat.
Add garlic and veal, browning each piece on both sides before adding in remaining ingredients (except for the corn starch). If pressure cooking set to high, secure the lid and cook for 6 minutes. If on the stove top, cover and simmer over medium heat for 20 minutes. Salt and pepper to taste and serve with pasta or potatoes. Drizzle with the cooking liquid and garnished with lemon. To thicken the cooking liquid into a heartier sauce: remove veal from pot setting aside under tin foil to keep warm. Combine 1 tablespoon cornstarch with 2 tablespoon water in a small dish and then stir into the pot, set to brown or over high heat, and simmer until thick. Return veal to pot and coat well with sauce before serving.

# TIP

*Many grocery stores sell thinly sliced veal scallopini, but you can always thin your own to 1/2 inch thickness by pounding with a mallet.*

# Veal Parmigiana

*The is the classic Italian-American veal dish.*
*Of course boneless chicken breasts can be substituted,*
*but veal has a different texture and flavor than chicken that can't be beat.*

**PREP TIME: 10 MINUTES**
**COOK TIME: 7 MINUTES**
**SERVES: 6**

## Ingredient List:

1 1/2 POUNDS THINLY SLICED VEAL, FROM THE LEG (SCALLOPINI) ABOUT SIX SLICES
1/2 CUP OLIVE OIL — *or a little more*
FLOUR, FOR DREDGING
PLAIN BREADCRUMBS, FOR DREDGING
2 EGGS
SALT AND FRESHLY GROUND BLACK PEPPER TO TASTE
1/2 CUP DRY WHITE WINE
JUICE OF 1 LEMON
MINCED FRESH PARSLEY LEAVES FOR GARNISH
1 LEMON, CUT INTO QUARTERS
2 CUPS CANNED TOMATO SAUCE MIXED WITH 1 TEASPOON OF VEGETABLE CONCENTRATE
1/2 CUP GRATED PARMESAN CHEESE
1 CUP MOZZARELLA CHEESE

## Cooking Instructions:

The cutlets should be less than 1/2 inch thick. If not: pound them gently between
two sheets of waxed paper. Heat the olive oil in a large skillet over medium heat,
while you set out the flour and bread crumbs on plates and beat the eggs lightly
in a small bowl. Season the flour liberally with salt and pepper. Set everything
near the stove. When the oil is good and hot, dredge the cutlets, one at a time in
the flour, then dip into the egg, then dredge in the bread crumbs. Add them to the
skillet, as they're ready. Cook them over medium high heat (don't crowd).
Cook in batches if necessary, adding additional oil as needed. Turn the cutlets as
soon as they're browned, then cook the other side. Total cooking time should be
4 minutes or less. As each piece of veal is done, place the cutlets in a baking dish
without overlapping (use two dishes if necessary). Top each with a spoonful or
two of the tomato sauce/Concentrate mixture and then with the Parmesan and
mozzarella. Put the baking dish in the oven and cook just until the cheese melts,
5 to 10 minutes. Serve immediately.

# TIP

*Don't overcook in the oven! If you want to brown the cheese,*
*under cook the veal in the skillet, about 3 total minutes. Then you can turn*
*the oven to broil. Watch carefully as the cheese will brown very fast!*

# Osso Buco

*If you have a pressure cooker this is the quintessential recipe for using it. With only 25 minutes cook time in a pressure cooker you may not even have enough time to make the gremolata\*— a lemon and herb topping that adds another dimension of flavor to an already extraordinary dish.*

PREP TIME: 15 MINUTES
COOK TIME: 25 MINUTES IN THE PRESSURE COOKER, 1 1/2 HOURS IN THE OVEN
SERVES: 4

## Ingredient List for Osso Buco:

3 TABLESPOONS OLIVE OIL
3-4 POUNDS VEAL SHANKS, 4 SHANKS CUT 1 TO 1 1/2 INCH THICK
1 CUP FLOUR, MIXED WITH 1/2 TEASPOON SALT AND 1/2 TEASPOON PEPPER
1 RED ONION, CHOPPED
2 TABLESPOONS GARLIC, MINCED
2 CARROTS, CUT INTO 1/2 INCH DISCS
2 STALKS CELERY, CHOPPED
1 TEASPOON CHICKEN CONCENTRATE MIXED INTO 1/2 CUP HOT WATER
1 CUP WHITE WINE
1 CAN DICED TOMATOES (14-16 OUNCES)
2 TABLESPOONS TOMATO PASTE
2 TEASPOONS ITALIAN SEASONING
SALT AND PEPPER TO TASTE

## Ingredient List for Gremolata\*:

1 TABLESPOON GARLIC, MINCED
1/2 CUP FRESH PARSLEY, CHOPPED
ZEST OF 1 LEMON
1/2 TEASPOON SALT

## Cooking Instructions:

Add the olive oil to a pressure cooker and heat on high or brown, or to a Dutch oven over medium high heat on the stove top. Dip veal shanks in seasoned flour until they are well coated and add to cooker or Dutch oven to lightly brown on both sides, remove and set aside. Deglaze\* with 1 cup of white wine. Add the garlic onion, carrots and celery and sauté for 1 minute before adding back veal and covering with the remaining Osso Buco ingredients. Set the pressure cooker to high, securely lock the lid and cook for 25 minutes. In a Dutch oven place in a 350 degree oven, cover and cook for 1 1/2 hours. While the Osso Buco is cooking, make the gremolata\* by combining all gremolata\* ingredients in a small bowl. When the Osso Buco is finished cooking, salt and pepper to taste. Serve topped with gremolata\*.

# TIP

*Serve over your favorite risotto for the true Italian presentation.*

# Olive Infused Lamb Chops with Red Wine

*This dish shouts out sunshine!*
*With very little effort you can picture yourself sitting on a*
*terrace overlooking the Mediterranean, sharing a meal with friends.*

PREP TIME: 15 MINUTES + I HOUR TO MARINATE
COOK TIME: 5 MINUTES IN THE PRESSURE COOKER, 20 MINUTES ON THE STOVETOP
SERVES: 6

## Ingredient List:

2 TABLESPOONS OLIVE OIL

1/4 CUP BLACK OLIVES, PITTED

2 TABLESPOONS GARLIC, MINCED

1 TEASPOON DRIED ROSEMARY

1 TEASPOON DRIED OREGANO

1 CUP DRY RED WINE MIXED WITH 1 TEASPOON OF VEGETABLE CONCENTRATE

6 LAMB CHOPS, 1/2 INCH THICK, TRIMMED OF EXCESS FAT

## Cooking Instructions:

Combine all ingredients (except lamb chops) in a blender or food processor
and blend until smooth to make a marinade. Cover lamb chops with marinade
in a large bowl or food storage container. Cover and refrigerate for at least
1 hour before cooking.

In a pressure cooker or heavy skillet add in 2 tablespoons of the marinade.
Add the lamb chops and lightly brown on both sides for about 2 to 3 minutes.
Cover chops with the remaining marinade and securely lock on the pressure
cooker lid. Set to high and cook for 5 minutes. If using a heavy skillet, cover
and simmer over medium heat for 20 minutes.

When done, remove chops and serve with a spoonful of cooking liquid
poured over top as a sauce.

# TIP

*Lighter side dishes go best with the strong flavors of the olive and wine.*
*Steamed vegetables and parsley or mashed potatoes*
*would make a wonderful meal.*

# SEAFOOD

# Lobster Newburg

*Lobster Newburg was first served in Delmonico's restaurant in New York City as Lobster Wenberg named after the sea captain who invented it. When a dispute arose over the recipe, the owner of Delmonico's changed "Wen" to "New." It is one of the few American dishes which have become a regular part of French cooking.*

**PREP TIME: 10 MINUTES**
**COOK TIME: 7 MINUTES**
**SERVES: 4**

### Ingredient List:

2 CUPS COOKED LOBSTER MEAT

3 TABLESPOONS BUTTER

1/2 TEASPOON SEAFOOD OR CHICKEN CONCENTRATE

3 TABLESPOON FLOUR

1 1/2 CUPS MILK

1 EGG YOLK, SLIGHTLY BEATEN

1 1/2 TABLESPOONS WHITE WINE

1/4 POUND MUSHROOMS, SLICED AND SAUTÉED IN 2 TBS BUTTER FOR 3 MINUTES

2 TABLESPOON PARSLEY, CHOPPED

### Cooking Instructions:

Melt butter and concentrate over low heat.

Add flour and pepper and stir one minute (until bubbly).

Remove from heat and stir in milk.

Return to heat stirring until mixture reaches a boil.

Combine half of the sauce with the egg yolk.

Return mixture to saucepan, stirring as you pour.

Add sherry, lobster meat and mushrooms.

Heat and serve garnished with parsley.

## TIP

*If you want to go back to the sweeter taste of the original Wenberg, use Sherry in place of the white wine, and add 2 tablespoons of Cognac.*

# Shrimp with Rum Glaze

PREP TIME: 10 MINUTES
COOK TIME: 8 MINUTES
SERVES: 4

## Ingredient List:

1/4 CUP HONEY

1/2 TEASPOON LIME JUICE

3 TABLESPOONS SPICED RUM

1 TABLESPOON VEGETABLE CONCENTRATE

1/2 TEASPOON GRATED ORANGE ZEST

1 TABLESPOON ORANGE JUICE

1 TEASPOON GRATED FRESH GINGER

1 TABLESPOON FRESH CILANTRO LEAVES, CHOPPED

1/4 TEASPOON SALT

1/4 TEASPOON GROUND BLACK PEPPER

1 1/2 TEASPOONS CORNSTARCH

20 JUMBO SHRIMP, PEELED AND DEVEINED

4 (10 INCH) SKEWERS

## Cooking Instructions:

Preheat an outdoor grill for medium heat, and lightly oil the grate.
Mix together the honey, lime juice, spiced rum, Vegetable Concentrate, orange zest,
orange juice, ginger, cilantro, salt, black pepper, and cornstarch in a large bowl
until the glaze is smooth and the cornstarch is thoroughly blended with the
rest of the ingredients. Pour half the glaze into a smaller bowl for basting.
Rinse and pat the shrimp dry, and gently stir into the large bowl to thoroughly
coat the shrimp with the glaze. Remove from the glaze, and discard the used glaze.
Thread 5 shrimp onto each skewer, and sprinkle with salt and black pepper.
Grill the shrimp until bright pink and the glaze has cooked onto the shrimp,
about 4 minutes per side. Baste with additional unused glaze before turning
the shrimp over.

# Chicken, Sausage and Shrimp Paella

*This was an award-winning recipe in a recipe contest a few years back.
...try it, you will love it!*

PREP TIME: 10 MINUTES
COOK TIME: 30 MINUTES
SERVES: 8 TO 10

## Ingredient List:

6 LINKS 1/4 POUND HOT ITALIAN SAUSAGE

7 (1 1/2 POUNDS) BONELESS, SKINLESS CHICKEN THIGHS, CUT INTO INCH SLICES

2 CUPS FRESH GREEN ONIONS, SLICED

4 CLOVES GARLIC, CRUSHED

1/2 TEASPOON OREGANO

2 TABLESPOONS CHICKEN CONCENTRATE MIXED WITH 6 CUPS OF WARM WATER

2 CUPS LONG-GRAIN RICE, UNCOOKED

3/4 TEASPOON SAFFRON THREADS

3 BAY LEAVES

1/4 CUP DRAINED PIMIENTO

5 TABLESPOONS FRESH PARSLEY, CHOPPED

3/4 POUNDS MEDIUM SHRIMP, PEELED AND DEVEINED

## Cooking Instructions:

Pierce sausage with a fork and place in microwave-safe covered casserole
with 1/2- inch of water. Microwave on high for 5 minutes or until center of
sausages lose their pinkness. Drain and cut into 3/4 inch slices.
Place sausage and chicken in a 4 quart Dutch oven.
Brown over medium heat, stirring occasionally.
Add onions, garlic, and oregano, and continue cooking until meat is browned.
Add Chicken Concentrate and water mixture and uncooked rice, stirring to
coat and blend all ingredients. Slowly stir in water. Add saffron and bay leaves.
Bring to a boil, reduce heat, and cover. Simmer for about 25 to 30 minutes.
Add pimiento, parsley and shrimp. Simmer for a few more minutes,
just until shrimp is cooked through.

# Dilled Almond Trout

*Dill is a common ingredient in salmon dishes.*
*The surprise is it's also great with trout.*

**PREP TIME: 10 MINUTES**
**COOK TIME: 20 TO 25 MINUTES**
**SERVES: 2**

## Ingredient List:

2 10 OUNCE TROUT, WHOLE

1/8 TEASPOON BLACK PEPPER

1/2 TEASPOON DILL

3/4 TEASPOON VEGETABLE CONCENTRATE MIXED WITH 1/2 CUP HOT WATER

1/3 CUP SLIVERED ALMONDS

LEMON WEDGES

## Cooking Instructions:

Place cleaned trout in shallow baking dish.
Mix pepper, dill and Vegetable Concentrate in water.
Pour over trout.
Sprinkle almonds over fish and bake at 350 degrees for 20 to 25 minutes,
or until fish flakes when touched with fork.
Season to taste with lemon and serve.

# TIP

*For a Springtime variation, add 1 cup of frozen peas cooked along with*
*1/4 chopped onion, 1 tablespoon of minced garlic and 1/4 cup of heavy cream.*
*Pour over the Trout.*

# Seared Salmon Supreme

*Salmon is one of those all-time favorite healthy meals for chefs to serve on their menus for many reasons; number one being that it's easy to prepare. Chefs don't like to take something this quick, easy, and delicious off the menu and after you try this recipe with a simple classic dill sauce neither will you!*

**PREP TIME: 10 MINUTES**
**COOK TIME: 6 MINUTES**
**SERVES: 4**

## Ingredient List:

1 TABLESPOON OLIVE OIL

1 TABLESPOON BUTTER — *may substitute olive or vegetable oil*

1 1/2 POUNDS SALMON, CUT INTO 4 SKINLESS FILLETS

1/4 TEASPOON SALT

1/4 TEASPOON PEPPER

1/2 FRESH LEMON

1/4 CUP WATER

1/4 CUP HEAVY CREAM

1 TEASPOON CHICKEN CONCENTRATE

1 1/2 TABLESPOONS FRESH DILL, CHOPPED — *may substitute 1 teaspoon dry*

1 TEASPOON DIJON MUSTARD

## Cooking Instructions:

Add the olive oil and butter to a large nonstick sauté pan over medium to high heat. Once hot, add salmon fillets and season the tops with salt and pepper. Cook salmon until bottom browns, about 2- 3 minutes, flip and squeeze the juice from the 1/2 lemon over the fillets. Add the water and continue cooking about 2 minutes more or until salmon is cooked and has a light pink color center. Remove salmon to a platter. Add heavy cream, Chicken Concentrate, dill and Dijon mustard to the pan and stir until thickened for sauce. Drape sauce over the salmon and serve garnished with fresh dill.

# TIP
### LIGHTEN UP THIS RECIPE
*Use 1/2 cup of reduced fat sour cream
in place of the heavy cream to lower the fat in the sauce.*

# Shrimp Creole

*If you are from New Orleans, you grew up with this delicious staple of Creole cooking. Here is a quick easy version that gets kicked up a notch with the chili powder.*

**PREP TIME: 10 MINUTES**
**COOK TIME: ABOUT ONE HOUR**
**SERVES: 4**

## Ingredient List:

1 SMALL GREEN BELL PEPPER, CHOPPED

1 SMALL BROWN ONION, CHOPPED

2 STALKS CELERY, CHOPPED

2 TABLESPOONS OLIVE OIL

1 CAN TOMATO SAUCE (8 OUNCE)

1 CAN CRUSHED TOMATOES (8 OUNCE)

1 TABLESPOON GARLIC POWDER

1 TABLESPOON BASIL, CHOPPED

1 TABLESPOON GUMBO FILET POWDER

1 TABLESPOON CHICKEN CONCENTRATE MIXED WITH 1/2 CUP OF WATER

1 1/2 CUP LARGE SHRIMP, PEELED AND DEVEINED

1 TABLESPOON CHILI POWDER

## Cooking Instructions:

In a large sauce pot, sauté bell pepper, onion and celery in olive oil, until onions turn translucent, about 3 minutes.
Add tomatoes, tomato sauce, spices, and Chicken Concentrate with water.
Simmer one hour and then add the shrimp and simmer an additional 5 minutes.
Serve over rice.

# TIP
*You can serve this dish over steamed vegetables or mashed potatoes.*

# BEANS
# & LEGUMES

# Italian White Bean Salad with Sausage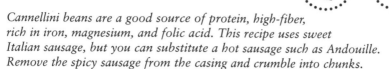

*Cannellini beans are a good source of protein, high-fiber,
rich in iron, magnesium, and folic acid. This recipe uses sweet
Italian sausage, but you can substitute a hot sausage such as Andouille.
Remove the spicy sausage from the casing and crumble into chunks.*

**PREP TIME: 15 MINUTES**
**COOK TIME: 20 MINUTES**
**SERVES: 6**

## Ingredient List:

1 Tablespoon olive oil

2 cans cannellini or white beans, drained and rinsed (15 ounce)

1/2 Pound Sweet Italian loose sausage

1 Tablespoon Chicken or Vegetable Concentrate added to 1/4 cup warm water

1 Tablespoon Balsamic Vinegar

3 cloves garlic, minced

1 tablespoon fresh basil, minced

1/4 teaspoon dry oregano

1 cup roasted red peppers, diced

1 Pinch of hot red pepper flakes — *optional*

salt and pepper to taste

## Cooking Instructions:

Over medium-high heat, add 1 tablespoon oil in a large deep skillet.
Add the Italian sausage and cook until browned. Drain any excess fat; add
the onions and garlic. Cook until onions are soft, about 2 minutes.
Pour stock in skillet and deglaze*. Add remaining ingredients; reduce
heat to low and simmer for 10 minutes, while stirring occasionally.
Salt and Pepper to taste.

# TIP

*To make this a vegan dish, omit the Italian sausage
and use Vegetable Concentrate instead of Chicken Concentrate.*

# Black-Eyed Pea Salad with Bacon & Bell Pepper

*This chilled black-eyed pea salad is a refreshing alternative to an Italian pasta salad for your next party or family get together. The soft black-eyed peas are complimented perfectly by the crunchy raw bell pepper and smoky bacon. It's a simple yet surprisingly new and unique picnic dish that is all prepped and ready to impress in minutes.*

**PREP TIME: 10 MINUTES**
**COOK TIME: 9 MINUTES IN A PRESSURE COOKER, ABOUT 20 MINUTES ON THE STOVETOP**
**SERVES: 8**

## Peas Ingredient List:

2 CUPS BLACK-EYED PEAS
2 TABLESPOONS VEGETABLE OIL, TO PREVENT FOAMING
1/2 TEASPOON GARLIC POWDER
1/2 TEASPOON ONION POWDER
1/2 TEASPOON ITALIAN SEASONING
1/4 TEASPOON GROUND BLACK PEPPER
1 TABLESPOON CHICKEN CONCENTRATE MIXED WITH WATER TO COVER BEANS

## Salad Ingredient List:

1 GREEN BELL PEPPER, CORED AND FINELY DICED
1 YELLOW BELL PEPPER, CORED AND FINELY DICED
1/2 CUP COOKED BACON PIECES — *available pre-cooked in salad dressing section*
1 CUP ROBUST ITALIAN SALAD DRESSING
2 TABLESPOONS MAYONNAISE
1/2 TEASPOON GROUND BLACK PEPPER
FRESH PARSLEY, FOR GARNISH — *optional*

## Cooking Instructions:

Combine the black-eyed peas, oil and spices in a pressure cooker or large saucepot. Add enough water to cover the beans. If pressure cooking securely lock on the pressure cooker's lid, set the cooker to high and cook for 9 minutes, then quick release the pressure. For the stove top bring to a boil, reduce heat and simmer for approximately 30 minutes or until beans are tender. The peas should be firm enough to hold up being mixed into the salad without turning into a mash. If too firm for your taste, cook for an additional few minutes. Drain the black-eyed peas into a colander and run cold water over them to cool down. Combine with all salad ingredients, stirring well. Cover and refrigerate for at least 2 hours before serving.

# TIP
*Though you can serve this as soon as it's chilled (or even as a warm salad), letting the salad marinate overnight really brings all of the flavors together in a truly great way, which is worth waiting for. Look for a good Italian dressing with plenty of spices and minced garlic at the bottom of the bottle for the best and fastest marinade.*

*This take on a Cuban classic is all mixed up... literally. So simple, yet
layered with flavors; serve this on its own as a vegetarian entrée or grill up some
chicken skewers to put on top. Throw a few sliced plantains on the grill for
close to an authentic Cuban meal.*

**PREP TIME: 10 MINUTES**
**COOK TIME: 4 MINUTES IN A PRESSURE COOKER, ABOUT 12 MINUTES ON THE STOVETOP**
**SERVES: 6**

## Ingredient List:

2 TABLESPOONS OLIVE OIL

1/2 ONION

1/2 GREEN BELL PEPPER, DICED

1 CAN BLACK BEANS (14-16OUNCES), WITH LIQUID

1 TEASPOON OREGANO

1/4 TEASPOON SUGAR

2 TEASPOONS CIDER VINEGAR

1/2 TEASPOON CHICKEN CONCENTRATE MIXED INTO 1/2 CUP OF WARM WATER

1/4 TEASPOON CUMIN

1/4 TEASPOON GARLIC POWDER

1 1/2 CUPS WATER

1 1/2 CUPS LONG GRAIN WHITE RICE, UNCOOKED

SALT AND PEPPER TO TASTE

## Cooking Instructions:

Add olive oil, onion and bell pepper to a pressure cooker or large saucepot.
Set cooker on brown, or stovetop to medium high, and sauté until onions are
almost completely translucent, about 4 minutes. Remove from heat.
Cover with the remaining ingredients (except for reserved water) and rice and stir
well to combine. Pat the mixture down softly with a spoon to even it out. Slowly
pour water over top the bean mixture without stirring. Then pour rice over top
everything. If pressure cooking, securely lock on the lid, set the cooker to high
and cook for 4 minutes. If on the stove top bring to a boil, then simmer for
approximately 15 minutes or until rice is tender. Let a pressure cooker release
naturally for 5 minutes and remove lid. After cooking let cool for 5 minutes for
rice to fluff up before serving.

# TIP
*You can serve this dish with a drizzle of balsamic vinegar over the top!*

# Curried Lentils

*Lentils are an inexpensive and protein packed legume that do not have
a very pronounced flavor of their own. This recipe gets a major boost in the
taste department with a good amount of curry. Serve them as a vegetarian entrée
or the perfect side for any meal that could use a little pick me up!*

**PREP TIME: 5 MINUTES**
**COOK TIME: 7 MINUTES IN A PRESSURE COOKER, ABOUT 30 MINUTES ON THE STOVETOP**
**SERVES: 6**

## Ingredient List:

2 CUPS DRIED LENTILS

2 TABLESPOONS VEGETABLE OIL

5 TEASPOONS CHICKEN CONCENTRATE MIXED INTO 5 CUPS WARM WATER

1 LARGE ONION, CHOPPED

1 TABLESPOON GARLIC, MINCED

2 TEASPOONS CURRY POWDER

1/4 TEASPOON TURMERIC

SALT TO TASTE

## Cooking Instructions:

Rinse lentils in a colander, picking through them to make sure there are
no stones or other objects that can be left behind in processing.
Add all ingredients to a pressure cooker or large saucepot.
If pressure cooking, lock lid in place and set to high and cook for 7 minutes.
On the stovetop bring to a boil, then simmer for 30 minutes or until lentils are tender.
When done simply salt to taste and serve.

# TIP

*For a spicier curry, try adding a teaspoon of chili powder and ground ginger.
For even spicier yet, throw in a pinch of cayenne pepper.*

# Honey Baked Beans

*This recipe for a BBQ and picnic staple uses honey instead of the molasses of more traditional baked beans. Just don't leave a batch lying around or a bee or two might bring the whole thing to their queen, bean by bean. Then they'd come for the burgers!*

**PREP TIME: 10 MINUTES**
**COOK TIME: 13 MINUTES IN A PRESSURE COOKER, ABOUT 35 MINUTES ON THE STOVETOP**
**SERVES: 6**

## Ingredient List:

1 POUND DRIED WHITE NAVY BEANS — *soaked for 6 hours!*

2 TABLESPOONS VEGETABLE OIL

WATER TO COVER BEANS

2 TABLESPOONS KETCHUP

1/4 CUP HONEY

1/2 CUP LIGHT BROWN SUGAR

1/2 TEASPOON GARLIC POWDER

1/2 TEASPOON ONION POWDER

1 TEASPOON VEGETABLE CONCENTRATE MIXED WITH 1 CUP OF HOT WATER

## Cooking Instructions:

Add the beans and vegetable oil to a pressure cooker or large stockpot or Dutch oven, and cover with water up to at least 1 1/2 inches above the beans. If pressure cooking, lock the lid and set to cook on high for ten minutes. If cooking on the stovetop, bring to a boil and then reduce heat and simmer for 35 minutes or until beans are tender. When done, drain beans. Return beans to pressure cooker or saucepot. Cover with the ketchup, honey, brown sugar, garlic powder, onion powder and water with Vegetable Concentrate, and stir well. If pressure-cooking, lock lid and cook for an additional 3 minutes on high. On the stovetop simmer for an additional ten minutes. In pressure cooker let pressure release naturally. When done serve or chill overnight and serve cold.

# TIP

*Replace the ketchup with a good BBQ sauce for beans with a bit more bang. Throw 1/4 cup of chopped raw bacon in with the beans just before cooking for something even better! Add sliced hot dogs with the ketchup for your childhood favorite.*

# Buttery Lima Beans with Sweet Bacon

*Believe it or not, this lima bean recipe is a real crowd pleaser.
With sweet brown sugar and savory bacon, lima beans don't even have
to be your cup of tea to enjoy this dish. And you may just find that
children will even eat a bean or two!*

PREP TIME: 5 MINUTES
COOK TIME: 5 MINUTES IN A PRESSURE COOKER, ABOUT 15 MINUTES ON THE STOVETOP
SERVES: 6

## Ingredient List:

2 TABLESPOONS BUTTER OR MARGARINE

2/3 CUP COOKED BACON PIECES — *sold precooked in salad dressing aisle*

1/2 RED ONION, DICED

1/4 CUP LIGHT BROWN SUGAR

1 BAG FROZEN LIMA BEANS (16 OUNCES)

1/2 TEASPOON VEGETABLE CONCENTRATE MIXED WITH 1/2 CUP HOT WATER

SALT AND PEPPER TO TASTE

## Cooking Instructions:

Add the butter, bacon and red onion to a pressure cooker or large saucepot.
Sauté for 3 to 4 minutes until onions begin to turn translucent.
Add brown sugar to bacon and onions and stir well.
Cover with lima beans and water and Concentrate mixture.
If pressure cooking, cook on high for 5 minutes. In a sauce pan, cook over
medium heat for about 15 minutes until beans are tender.
When done, salt and pepper to taste and serve.

# TIP

*Some people prefer this with the smaller "baby lima beans"
but it can be made with any lima or butter bean,
or pretty much any variety of frozen bean for that matter!*

# VEGETABLES
# & SIDE DISHES

# Italian Chicken Spring Rolls

*This recipe combines traditional Italian ingredients with an Oriental wonton wrapper. An Oritalia recipe of East meets West.*

**PREP TIME: 10 MINUTES**
**COOK TIME: 12 MINUTES**
**SERVES: 6**

## Ingredient List:

2 POUNDS SKINNED CHICKEN BREAST, FINELY DICED

1 CUP YELLOW ONION, DICED

1 CUP RED ROASTED PEPPERS, DICED

2 TABLESPOONS MINCED GARLIC

1 PACKAGE SMALL WONTON SKINS (4 INCHES)

1 CUP OLIVE OIL

1 TABLESPOON CHICKEN CONCENTRATE

1/2 TEASPOON FRESHLY GROUND PEPPER

8 OUNCES MOZZARELLA CHEESE, SHREDDED

1/2 TEASPOON DRIED BASIL

1 CUP SHITAKE MUSHROOMS, STEMS REMOVED, DICED

## Cooking Instructions:

In a large saucepan, over medium heat, add 4 tablespoons of oil.
Sauté chicken and onion in the oil for 5 minutes, stirring occasionally.
Reduce heat to simmer. Add roasted peppers, garlic and Chicken Concentrate.
Stir and allow mixture to simmer another 2 minutes.
Turn off heat, stir dried basil and mozzarella, and allow mixture to cool.
Per directions on wonton skin package, spoon approximatcly 1 tablespoon chicken mixture onto the middle of each skin and fold over, pressing edges until they stick together. Place rolls on slightly greased cookie sheet allowing 1 inch between rolls. Preheat oven to 375 degrees.
Place cookie sheet in oven and bake for 10-12 minutes.

## TIP

*Serve with one of the Great Flavors sauces. Options include:*
*Cabernet Cream Sauce, Mushroom Bordelaise, Marsala Sauce,*
*Vodka Sauce, Au Poivre Sauce or Chablis Sauce.*

# Roasted Vegetables

PREP TIME: 10 MINUTES
COOK TIME: 35 MINUTES
SERVES: 2-4

## Ingredient List:

2 MEDIUM POTATOES, PEELED AND CUT INTO 1/2-INCH CUBES

2 MEDIUM CARROTS, CUT INTO 1/2-INCH SLICES

1 LARGE ZUCCHINI, CUT INTO 1/2-INCH PIECES

1 LARGE SWEET RED PEPPER, CUT INTO 1-INCH PIECES

2 TABLESPOONS OLIVE OR VEGETABLE OIL

2 TABLESPOONS VEGETABLE CONCENTRATE

1 TEASPOON DRIED BASIL

1 TEASPOON DRIED OREGANO

1/2 TEASPOON SALT — *optional*

1/4 TEASPOON PEPPER

2 GARLIC CLOVES, MINCED

1/2 CUP PARMESAN CHEESE, GRATED

## Cooking Instructions:

In a mixing bowl, combine the potatoes, carrots, zucchini and red pepper.
Combine the remaining ingredients; drizzle over vegetables.
Stir to coat.
Transfer to an ungreased 13x9x2-inch baking dish.
Bake, uncovered, at 375 degrees for 30-35 minutes or until tender.
Remove from oven and top with Parmesan cheese before serving.

# TIP

*Roasted veggies keep well in the refrigerator for 3-5 days.*
*They make a great anti-pasta for any meal.*

# Ratatouille

*This is another classic French recipe with a million variations to be made. Though it may seem like a lot of work at first, this is one of the easiest ratatouilles you'll find and at only 6 minutes under pressure, it's most certainly the fastest!*

PREP TIME: 20 MINUTES
COOK TIME: 6 MINUTES IN A PRESSURE COOKER, ABOUT 45 MINUTES ON THE OVEN
SERVES: 6

## Ingredient List:

4 TABLESPOONS OLIVE OIL

2 TABLESPOONS GARLIC, MINCED

1 LARGE ONION, QUARTERED, THEN THINLY SLICED

2 TABLESPOONS TOMATO PASTE

1 EGGPLANT, CUT INTO 1 INCH CUBES

1 GREEN BELL PEPPER, CUT INTO 1/2 INCH SQUARE PIECES

1 RED BELL PEPPER, CUT INTO 1/2 INCH SQUARE PIECES

1 LARGE ZUCCHINI, CHOPPED LARGE

1 LARGE YELLOW SQUASH, CHOPPED LARGE

2 TOMATOES, CHOPPED LARGE

2 TEASPOONS ITALIAN SEASONING

1 TEASPOON SALT

1/2 TEASPOON GROUND BLACK PEPPER

1 TEASPOON VEGETABLE CONCENTRATE MIXED INTO 1/2 CUP OF HOT WATER

PARMESAN CHEESE FOR GARNISH — *optional*

## Cooking Instructions:

Add the olive oil and garlic to a pressure cooker or Dutch oven.
Set to brown in pressure cooker or on the stove top until sizzling.
Add the onions and cook until they begin to sweat and turn translucent.
Add the tomato paste and stir to thin it out. Add remaining ingredients, pouring the vegetable broth over the top last. If pressure cooking, lock on the lid, set the cooker to low and cook for 6 minutes, then quick release the pressure.
In a Dutch oven, cover and bake in a 350 degree oven for approximately 45 minutes. Serve warm with freshly grated, shredded or shaved Parmesan cheese

# TIP

*There is much debate over when ratatouille is at its best, either immediately after preparing, while some flavors are still separate or refrigerated overnight when the flavors have melded together. You decide!*

# Portobella Mushroom with Sundried Tomato Sauce

*These mushrooms are rich in flavor and meaty in texture.*
*Along with the infused Beef Concentrate sauce you may think*
*you are eating a prime filet!*

**PREP TIME: 15 MINUTES**
**COOK TIME: 10 MINUTES**
**SERVES: 6**

## Ingredient List:

3 LARGE PORTOBELLA MUSHROOMS (AT LEAST 4 INCH DIAMETER)

1 TEASPOON BEEF CONCENTRATE

1 TABLESPOON BUTTER

1/4 CUP EXTRA VIRGIN OLIVE OIL

1/2 CUP HEAVY CREAM

1/2 CUP DICED SHALLOTS

2 TABLESPOONS MINCED FRESH BASIL

1/4 TEASPOON FRESHLY GROUND WHITE PEPPER

1/2 CUP ROASTED RED PEPPERS, DICED

1/2 CUP SUNDRIED TOMATOES, DICED

1/2 CUP BLUE CHEESE CRUMBLES (OPTIONAL) — *optional*

## Cooking Instructions:

Rinse mushrooms. Lay mushrooms flat on a cutting board and slice them
into 1/2 inch strips. Brush mushroom strips with olive oil and set aside.
Heat 1 tablespoon olive oil in a large deep skillet over medium heat.
Place mushrooms in skillet, making sure they lie flat. Cook mushrooms for
2 minutes on each side. Remove mushrooms and place on a serving dish.
Set heat to simmer, add butter, shallots, sundried tomatoes and let simmer
for 2 minutes. Add red peppers and stir. Add heavy cream, Beef Concentrate,
ground pepper and basil. Stir for an additional minute, and remove from heat.
Spoon sundried tomato sauce onto Portobello mushrooms and serve warm
Top with the blue cheese crumbles, if desired.

# Vegetable Quiche with Bacon and Cheese

**PREP TIME: 15 MINUTES**
**COOK TIME: 45 MINUTES**
**SERVES: 6-8**

## Ingredient List:

1/4 POUND FRESH ASPARAGUS, TRIMMED AND CUT INTO 1/2 INCH PIECES

1/4 POUND RED PEPPERS

1/4 POUND FRESH BROCCOLI

1/4 POUND RED ONIONS, DICED

10 SLICES BACON

2 (8 INCH) UNBAKED PIE SHELLS

1 EGG WHITE, LIGHTLY BEATEN

4 EGGS

1 1/2 CUPS HALF-AND-HALF CREAM

1/4 TEASPOON GROUND NUTMEG

SALT AND PEPPER TO TASTE

1 TABLESPOON VEGETABLE CONCENTRATE

2 CUPS SWISS CHEESE, SHREDDED

## Cooking Instructions:

Preheat oven to 400 degrees. Place fresh vegetables in a steamer over 1 inch
of boiling water, and cover. Cook until tender but still firm, about 2 to 6 minutes.
Drain and cool. Place bacon in a large, deep skillet. Cook over medium high heat
or in oven at 350 degrees until evenly brown. Drain, crumble and set aside.
Brush pie shells with beaten egg white. Sprinkle crumbled bacon and chopped
vegetables into pie shells. In a bowl, beat together eggs, cream, nutmeg, vegetable
concentrate, salt and pepper. Sprinkle Swiss cheese over bacon and asparagus.
Pour egg mixture on top of cheese. Bake uncovered in preheated oven until firm,
about 35 to 40 minutes. Let cool to room temperature before serving.

## TIP

*Serve this for breakfast with a side of sliced tomatoes sprinkled with*
*finely chopped basil and a drizzle of balsamic vinegar.*

# Bacon Duxelle Stuffed Mushrooms

*You can't help but find French influence in cooking everywhere, especially New Orleans. These Cajun beauties mingle the French cooking philosophy of not wasting food by using the entire mushroom with the southern philosophy that adding bacon to most anything makes it better!*

PREP TIME: 15 MINUTES
COOK TIME: 15 MINUTES
SERVES: 4

## Ingredient List:

VEGETABLE OIL SPRAY

16 OUNCES MEDIUM WHITE BUTTON MUSHROOMS

5 LARGE SLICES RAW BACON, CHOPPED

1 TABLESPOON RED ONION, MINCED

1 OUNCE SHERRY — *may substitute 1/2 teaspoon of Worcestershire sauce*

1/2 TEASPOON MUSHROOM OR CHICKEN CONCENTRATE

1 TEASPOON FRESH CHOPPED TARRAGON

1/8 TEASPOON SALT

1/8 TEASPOON BLACK PEPPER

1 GREEN ONION, THINLY SLICED FOR GARNISH — *optional*

## Cooking Instructions:

Preheat the oven to 350 degrees and spray a baking pan with vegetable oil spray. Wipe mushrooms clean, twist off the stems (save) and place the caps on the baking sheet. Chop the stems finely and set aside.

In a large sauté pan over medium-high heat add the bacon and cook until crispy. Add the chopped mushroom stems and remaining ingredients (except green onion) and continue to cook until liquid is evaporated and stems are tender.

Remove from heat. Stuff each cap with a rounded spoonful of stuffing. Place back on the baking sheet and bake for 15 minutes or until mushrooms are tender. Serve hot topped with sliced green onion if desired.

# TIP

*A food processor or mini chopper makes short work of mincing anything. In this recipe you may add the mushroom stems and red onion together, mince and then add to the recipe as one!*

# RICE
# & RISOTTO

# Cherry Tomato Risotto

*Though you can pretty much put anything in or on top of a risotto and it will be delicious; there is definitely something special to a pan seared cherry tomato. Serve it topped with a juicy grilled steak and you're in business!*

PREP TIME: 10 MINUTES
COOK TIME: 7 MINUTES
SERVES: 4

## Ingredient List:

1 TABLESPOON OLIVE OIL

2 TABLESPOONS BUTTER OR MARGARINE

1 TABLESPOON MINCED GARLIC

2 1/2 CUPS CHERRY TOMATOES, HALVED

2 CUPS ARBORIO RICE, UNCOOKED

4 TEASPOONS CHICKEN CONCENTRATE MIXED INTO 6 CUPS OF WARM WATER

1 TABLESPOON DRY RED WINE

1 TABLESPOON CHOPPED FRESH BASIL

1/4 CUP PARMESAN CHEESE, SHREDDED

SALT AND PEPPER TO TASTE

## Cooking Instructions:

Add the oil, butter, garlic and 2 cup of the cherry tomato halves (reserving the other 1/2 cup for garnish) to a pressure cooker or large saucepot. Heat on brown for pressure cooker or medium heat in saucepot, stirring constantly until sizzling. Add the rice and stir constantly for 1 minute to coat with the oil and butter. Add remaining ingredients (except for Parmesan cheese) stir and if using a pressure cooker, lock on the lid set to high and cook for 7 minutes. On the stovetop bring to a boil and simmer until all of the liquid is absorbed, about 15 to twenty minutes, stirring every so often until the rice is tender. Add more water if necessary, up to several more cups as water will evaporate with stove top cooking. When done, serve topped with reserved cherry tomato halves and shredded Parmesan cheese.

## TIP

*Stir in a cup of thawed frozen corn kernels right before serving, letting sit for 2 minutes to warm through for an extra sweet burst of flavor that both complements and contrasts the cherry tomatoes.*

# Wild Rice Almondine

*This wild rice dish is reminiscent of the holidays. Though the dried cranberries are optional, they are highly recommended if you're cooking up poultry. The cranberries and almonds lend a sweet contrast to an otherwise savory side that will all but make the meal!*

PREP TIME: 5 MINUTES
COOK TIME: 25 MINUTES IN A PRESSURE COOKER, ABOUT 45 MINUTES ON THE STOVETOP
SERVES: 4

## Ingredient List:

1 CUP WILD RICE, DRY

3 TABLESPOONS BUTTER OR MARGARINE

3 1/2 TEASPOONS CHICKEN CONCENTRATE MIXED INTO 3 1/2 CUPS WARM WATER

1/2 TEASPOON GARLIC POWDER

1/2 TEASPOON ONION POWDER

1 CUP LONG GRAIN WHITE RICE, UNCOOKED

3/4 CUP BLANCHED ALMOND SLIVERS — *sold in the baking isle*

1 TABLESPOON PARSLEY FLAKES

1/2 CUP DRIED CRANBERRIES — *optional*

SALT AND PEPPER TO TASTE

## Cooking Instructions:

Rinse wild rice thoroughly before cooking.

Add the butter, chicken concentrate mix, garlic powder, and onion powder to a pressure cooker or large saucepot. In the pressure cooker set to high and cook for 20 minutes. On the stovetop bring to boil and then set to low and cook, undisturbed, for 40 minutes. With pressure cooker, quick release steam. Stir in the white rice and almond slivers. If pressure cooking, lock on lid, set to high and cook for an additional 5 minutes. On the stovetop, cook for an additional 10 minutes. When done immediately stir in the parsley flakes and dried cranberries. Let the rice sit for 5 minutes to fluff up as cranberries soften slightly. Salt and pepper to tastes and serve.

# Portobella Risotto

PREP TIME: 10 MINUTES
COOK TIME: 7 MINUTES IN PRESSURE COOKER, 20 MINUTES ON STOVE TOP
SERVES: 4

## Ingredient List:

1 TABLESPOON OLIVE OIL

2 TABLESPOONS BUTTER OR MARGARINE

1/2 RED ONION, DICED

2 LARGE PORTOBELLA MUSHROOM CAPS, CHOPPED

2 CUPS ARBORIO RICE, UNCOOKED

1 TABLESPOON VEGETABLE CONCENTRATE MIXED WITH 6 CUPS OF HOT WATER

1/2 CUP DRY RED WINE

2 TEASPOONS DRIED THYME

1/4 CUP PARMESAN CHEESE, GRATED

SALT AND PEPPER TO TASTE

## Cooking Instructions:

Place oil, butter, onion and chopped portobella mushrooms in a pressure cooker
or large saucepot. Brown, stirring constantly for 2 minutes, until mushrooms
begin to cook down. Add rice and stir constantly for 1 minute to coat with oil.
Add remaining ingredients except for the Parmesan cheese.
If pressure cooking, lock on lid and set cooker to high for 7 minutes.
If in a saucepan, bring to boil and then simmer stirring often until liquid is
absorbed. Add additional water if necessary to achieve desired doneness.
Stir in Parmesan cheese, salt and pepper to taste and serve immediately.

## TIP

*If you like your mushrooms al dente,*
*set them aside before adding the rice to the pot.*
*Stir them into the risotto when it is done cooking.*
*Let the mushrooms warm in the risotto for 2 minutes before serving.*

# Risotto with Gorgonzola and Walnuts

*There is no better complement to a creamy risotto than a good quality, creamy Gorgonzola cheese. Try garnishing this with diced red apples to take this recipe to a whole different place. It's like a warm Waldorf salad and risotto all in one! The sweet apple perfectly contrasts the earthy walnuts and strong Gorgonzola cheese.*

PREP TIME: 5 MINUTES
COOK TIME: 7 MINUTES IN PRESSURE COOKER, 20 MINUTES ON STOVETOP
SERVES: 6

## Ingredient List:

1 TABLESPOON OLIVE OIL

2 TABLESPOONS BUTTER OR MARGARINE

1 ONION, DICED

2 CUPS ARBORIO RICE, UNCOOKED

1 TABLESPOON VEGETABLE CONCENTRATE MIXED WITH 6 CUPS OF HOT WATER

1 CUP DRY WHITE WINE

1/4 CUP PARMESAN CHEESE, GRATED

6 OUNCES GORGONZOLA CHEESE CRUMBLES

1/2 CUP WALNUTS, CHOPPED

SALT AND PEPPER TO TASTE

1 RED APPLE, DICED FOR GARNISH — *optional*

## Cooking Instructions:

Add the oil, butter and diced onion to the pressure cooker or large saucepan and heat on high or brown stirring constantly until sizzling. Add rice and stir constantly for 1 minute to coat with oil. Add vegetable broth and white wine. If pressure cooking, lock on lid and set cooker to high for 7 minutes. If in a saucepan, bring to boil and then simmer stirring often until liquid is absorbed. Add additional water if necessary to achieve desired doneness. Stir in Gorgonzola and Parmesan cheese and chopped walnuts. Salt and pepper to taste, garnish with apple and serve immediately.

# TIP
*Toasted walnuts work best in this risotto.*
*If you can only find raw walnuts, preheat the oven to*
*350 degrees and place raw walnuts on a sheet pan, single layer.*
*Bake for 10 minutes or until you can smell the walnuts toasting.*

# Authentic Spanish Rice

*Today, Spanish rice is often made with a variety of garden vegetables in addition to the traditional, tomatoes, onions and garlic.*
*If you want the original, this is it! You can always add more veggies.*

**PREP TIME: 5 MINUTES**
**COOK TIME: 20 MINUTES**
**SERVES: 4**

### Ingredient List:

1 CUP LONG-GRAIN WHITE RICE, UNCOOKED

1/2 SMALL ONION, FINELY CHOPPED

2 TABLESPOONS VEGETABLE OIL

1 TABLESPOONS CHICKEN CONCENTRATE DISSOLVED IN 2 1/2 CUPS HOT WATER

4 OUNCES TOMATO SAUCE

1 TABLESPOON GARLIC, MINCED

### Cooking Instructions:

In a sauté pan cook rice and onion in vegetable oil over medium high heat until golden brown. Add chicken concentrate, tomato sauce, salt and garlic to the pan. Cook over low heat until water evaporates (approximately 20 minutes). Serve as side dish or complete meal by adding any sautéed meat such as chicken fingers or beef strips.

## TIP

*Add 1/4 cup each of additional chopped and cooked veggies in season for a different Spanish rice.*

*Pilaf refers to any dish that is prepared with a grain and then cooked or baked with oil before being cooked with a seasoned broth. Rice pilaf includes rice. It may also include meat and other vegetables, though the type and seasoning vary by region. Onions, carrots, peas and potatoes are popular options as are mutton, beef and chicken. The rice that it incorporates can also vary from basmati rice to brown rice.*

**PREP TIME: 5 MINUTES**
**COOK TIME: 20 MINUTES**
**SERVES: 6**

### Ingredient List:

1 CUP LONG-GRAIN WHITE RICE, UNCOOKED

1 SMALL ONION, FINELY CHOPPED

1 CUP CELERY, CHOPPED

1 TEASPOON CHOPPED PARSLEY

2 TABLESPOONS VEGETABLE OIL

1 TABLESPOON CHICKEN CONCENTRATE DISSOLVED IN 2 1/2 CUPS HOT WATER

### Cooking Instructions:

In a sauté pan cook rice celery and onion in vegetable oil over medium high heat until golden brown. Add chicken concentrate and water, parsley and salt to the pan. Cook over low heat until water evaporates (approximately 20 minutes). Serve as side dish or complete meal by adding any sautéed meat such as chicken fingers or beef strips.

## TIP

*Add 1/4 cup each of additional chopped and cooked veggies in season for a alternative Rice Pilaf.*

# Couscous with Pine Nuts and Raisins

*This recipe for Couscous is a typical Moroccan preparation with chopped raisins or dried fruit and cinnamon adding slight sweetness to this otherwise savory dish. For the best results, keep an eye out for regular uncooked couscous not the instant variety that comes in a box.*

**PREP TIME: 10 MINUTES**
**COOK TIME: 10 MINUTES**
**SERVES: 8**

## Ingredient List:

1 TABLESPOON VEGETABLE CONCENTRATE STIRRED INTO 2 1/4 CUPS HOT WATER

1 CINNAMON STICK

5 CARDAMOM PODS

SALT AND PEPPER TO TASTE

1/3 CUP RAISINS — *or minced dried fruit such as figs, apricots, dates or a combination*

1/2 CUP HOT WATER

4 TABLESPOONS BUTTER (1/2 STICK)

1/2 CUP PINE NUTS

1 1/2 CUPS COUSCOUS, DRY

MINCED FRESH PARSLEY OR CILANTRO LEAVES FOR GARNISH — *optional*

## Cooking Instructions:

In a small saucepan, warm the 2 1/4 cups vegetable stock with the cinnamon, cardamom, salt, and pepper while you prepare the other ingredients.
Soak the raisins or dried fruit in the 1/2 cup hot water.
Place 1 tablespoon butter in a small skillet and turn the heat to medium. When it melts, add the pine nuts and cook, stirring occasionally, until they brown lightly, about 5 minutes. Set aside.
Place 2 tablespoons butter in a medium saucepan and turn the heat to medium-low. When it melts, add the couscous and cook, stirring, until it is coated with butter, about 1 minute. Strain the stock or water and add it all at once. Bring to a boil, and then turn the heat down to its minimum.
Cover and cook until all the liquid is absorbed, 5 to 8 minutes.
Drain the raisins or fruit and gently stir them in, along with the pine nuts and remaining butter. Fluff with a fork to break up any lumps. Garnish and serve.

# TIP

*Like polenta, couscous is best served with savory stews, whether meat or vegetable.*

# Asparagus Risotto

*There is something about the combination of Asparagus and Risotto,
that make this the most popular risotto recipe in the world.*

**PREP TIME: 10 MINUTES**
**COOK TIME: 7 MINUTES IN PRESSURE COOKER, 20 MINUTES ON STOVETOP**
**SERVES: 6**

## Ingredient List:

1 POUND FRESH ASPARAGUS
1 TABLESPOON MINCED GARLIC
2 TABLESPOONS BUTTER OR MARGARINE
2 CUPS ARBORIO RICE, UNCOOKED
1 TABLESPOON VEGETABLE CONCENTRATE MIXED WITH 6 CUPS OF WATER
1 CUP DRY WHITE WINE
1 TEASPOON LEMON JUICE
1/4 CUP PARMESAN CHEESE, GRATED OR SHREDDED
SALT AND PEPPER TO TASTE

## Cooking Instructions:

Trim about 1 1/2 inches of the bottom, tough end of the asparagus and discard.
Trim off the asparagus tips, about 1 1/2 inches from the top and place into a
microwave safe dish. You should be left with the middle section of the asparagus
stalks. Chop the stalks into 1/2 inch lengths. Add the oil, butter and minced garlic
to a large saucepot and heat for a couple of minutes or until butter is melted.
Add the rice and stir to coat the grains. Add the asparagus stalks, Vegetable
Concentrate, wine and lemon juice. In a pressure cooker lock lid in place and set
on high for 7 minutes, and quick release the pressure. On the stovetop bring to boil
over medium high heat and stir every few minutes, adding additional water if needed
stirring until rice is tender and creamy, about 20 minutes. While the risotto is cooking,
add water to the microwave safe dish of asparagus tips, enough that they are
completely submerged. Microwave for 2 to 3 minutes until tips are tender but not
mushy. Drain water. When risotto is done, stir in the Parmesan cheese and asparagus tips.
Salt and pepper to taste and serve immediately.

# TIP

*Most asparagus is shrink wrapped in a foam tray and the easiest way to cut
the crunchy and inedible bottoms off is to place the wrapped foam tray on a cutting
board and carefully chop through the entire package and all stalks in one swipe.*

# PASTA

# Pasta Primavera

*This classic pasta is a world-wide favorite and a great way to use seasonal veggies or just any that may be hanging out in your fridge. Simply slice and dice, throw them in a pan and you'll be serving a healthy colorful gourmet dinner in no time at all!*

PREP: 15 MINUTES
COOK: 15 MINUTES
SERVES: 4

## Ingredient List:

8 OUNCES WHOLE WHEAT PENNE PASTA, UNCOOKED — *may use ziti or similar*

2 TABLESPOONS OLIVE OIL

1 CUP YELLOW SQUASH, HALVED AND CUT INTO 1/2 INCH SLICES

1 CUP ZUCCHINI, HALVED AND CUT INTO 1/2 INCH SLICES

1 CUP RED BELL PEPPER STRIPS — *may use any color pepper*

1 TEASPOON GARLIC, MINCED

1/2 CUP WATER

1 TEASPOON VEGETABLE CONCENTRATE

1 TABLESPOON FRESH BASIL LEAVES, CHIFFONADE*— *may use 1 teaspoon of dry basil*

10 CHERRY TOMATOES, HALVED

1/4 TEASPOON SALT

1/4 TEASPOON CRACKED BLACK PEPPER

1/4 CUP GRATED PARMESAN CHEESE — *optional*

## Cooking Instructions:

Bring a stock pot with salted water to a boil and cook pasta until just tender. Drain, rinse and set aside.

In a large sauté pan over high heat add the oil, squash, zucchini and pepper strips. Cook for 3 minutes until tender but crisp.

Add the remaining ingredients and bring to a simmer.

Stir in the tomatoes and cooked pasta and heat for another minute.

Serve topped with grated Parmesan cheese and sprigs of fresh basil if desired.

# TIP
*Replace the water with heavy cream and add cooked chicken or ham for a hearty family meal!*

# Ratatouille Pasta

PREP TIME: 5 MINUTES + 30 MNIUTES STANDING TIME
COOK TIME: 10 MINUTES
SERVES: 4

## Ingredient List:

2 CUPS EGGPLANT, PEELED AND DICED

2 CUPS ZUCCHINI, SLICED

1/2 TEASPOON SALT

1 1/3 CUPS SPIRAL PASTA, UNCOOKED

1 CUP ONION, SLICED

1 TABLESPOON OLIVE OIL

1 CAN DICED TOMATOES, UNDRAINED (14.5 OUNCE)

2 TABLESPOONS TOMATO PASTE

2 TABLESPOONS VEGETABLE CONCENTRATE

1 TEASPOON DRIED OREGANO

1/2 TEASPOON GARLIC POWDER

1/2 TEASPOON DRIED BASIL

DASH PEPPER

1 CUP SHREDDED PART-SKIM MOZZARELLA CHEESE

## Cooking Instructions:

Place eggplant and zucchini in a colander over a plate; sprinkle with salt and toss.
Let stand for 30 minutes; rinse and drain well.
Cook pasta according to package directions.
Meanwhile, in a large nonstick skillet, saute the eggplant, zucchini and onion
in oil until tender. Add the tomatoes, tomato paste, Vegetable Concentrate, oregano,
garlic powder, basil and pepper. Bring to a boil. Reduce heat; cook, uncovered,
over medium-low heat for 3 minutes, stirring occasionally.
Drain pasta; place on an ovenproof platter. Top with vegetable mixture.
Sprinkle with mozzarella cheese. Broil 4-6 inches from the heat until cheese is melted.

# TIP

*For a more complex dish, add a chopped bell pepper and a large diced carrot.*

# Orzo Primavera

*This light and refreshing pasta dish with a bevy of beautiful, brightly colored vegetables may just remind you of Spring. It's no coincidence, as that's where Primavera gets its name! The small, almost rice sized orzo pasta is yet another breath of fresh air when you're tired of ordinary rice or pasta.*

**PREP TIME: 10 MINUTES**
**COOK TIME: 8 MINUTES**
**SERVES 6**

### Ingredient List:

1 TABLESPOON BUTTER

2 TABLESPOONS OLIVE OIL

1 TEASPOON MINCED GARLIC

1/2 RED ONION, DICED

1 1/2 CUP ORZO, UNCOOKED — *sold in the pasta isle*

3 TEASPOONS VEGETABLE CONCENTRATE MIXED INTO 3 CUPS WATER

1 TABLESPOON LEMON JUICE

1 1/2 TEASPOONS GROUND CINNAMON

SALT AND PEPPER TO TASTE

### Cooking Instructions:

Place the oil, onion, bell pepper and dates in a large sauce pan and heat on medium high heat stirring constantly for 2-3 minutes until onions are sweating and translucent. Add remaining ingredients. Bring to boil, then simmer for 4 minutes. Salt and pepper to taste and serve.

# TIP

*If you like a bit of a kick, try adding 1/2 teaspoon of cayenne pepper before cooking. This dish makes a nice presentation when garnished with chopped pecans or toasted almonds.*

# Penne Alla Vodka

*This pasta has had a little too much to drink and now it's blushing!*
*An American Italian classic, Penne Alla Vodka combines a red and white sauce*
*with a shot of its namesake vodka for a distinctive flavor that's a knock-out*
*punch guaranteed to leave you punch-drunk!*

**PREP TIME: 5 MINUTES**
**COOK TIME: 12 MINUTES**
**SERVES: 6**

## Ingredient List:

3 CUPS PENNE PASTA, UNCOOKED

1 TEASPOON VEGETABLE CONCENTRATE stirred into 1 1/2 CUPS OF HOT WATER

1 JAR OF STORE BOUGHT MARINARA SAUCE (24-26OUNCES)

1 CAN DICED TOMATOES (14-16 OUNCES)

2 TABLESPOONS BUTTER OR MARGARINE

2 TEASPOONS MINCED GARLIC

1 1/4 CUP VODKA

1/2 CUP HEAVY CREAM

1/4 CUP PARMESAN CHEESE

SALT AND PEPPER TO TASTE

## Cooking Instructions:

Add all ingredients, except heavy cream and Parmesan cheese into a large saucepot set to medium high heat. Bring to boil and then simmer for 12 minutes until penne is tender. Stir in the heavy cream and Parmesan cheese until melted and creamy. Salt and pepper to taste and serve immediately.

# TIP
*If you really want to kick this dish up a notch,*
*try sauteing 1/2 cup of diced bacon before step 1 in the recipe.*

# Cheese Tortellini Alfredo with Ham

*When you're feeding the whole family, this is a grown up dish that the kids are guaranteed to love. And with so little prep time, it's something you can literally whip together in only ten minutes ...another good thing when feeding a whole family!*

PREP TIME: 5 MINUTES
COOK TIME: 8 MINUTES
SERVES: 6

## Tortellini Ingredient List:

1 LARGE BAG CHEESE TORTELLINI, DRY (13 OUNCES) — *sold in the pasta aisle*

1 1/2 CUPS CUBED OR DICED HAM — *sold already cubed in most stores*

1 TEASPOON VEGETABLE CONCENTRATE STIRRED INTO 2 1/2 CUPS WARM WATER

3 TABLESPOONS BUTTER OR MARGARINE

1/2 TEASPOON GARLIC POWDER

1/4 TEASPOON GROUND BLACK PEPPER

1/8 TEASPOON NUTMEG

## Dairy Ingredient List:

3/4 CUP GRATED PARMESAN CHEESE

3/4 CUP WHOLE MILK

4 OUNCES CREAM CHEESE (1/2 REGULAR SIZED BRICK)

SALT TO TASTE

## Cooking Instructions:

Add all Tortellini ingredients to saucepot over high heat and bring to boil, then lower heat and simmer for 8 minutes or until tortellini is tender.
Stir in the dairy ingredients until melted and creamy.
Salt and pepper to taste and serve immediately.

# TIP

*If the sauce is too thin, add more cream cheese until you get the right consistency. If it is too thick, just add more milk. Go full Italian by replacing the cubed ham with cooked, diced pancetta or try 2/3 cup of a precooked bacon pieces, sold in the sold dressing aisle.*

# Angel Hair Pasta
## with Bordelaise Butter Cream Sauce

*You don't normally think of brown sauce on pasta but it's been going on for centuries! All but forgotten, a dish like this can only be found these days at a handful of high-end restaurants. And that's exactly what your kitchen will be as this easy recipe instantly brings world class flavor to your table!*

**PREP TIME: 5 MINUTES**
**COOK TIME: 15 MINUTES**
**SERVES: 4**

### Ingredient List:

8 OUNCES ANGEL HAIR PASTA, UNCOOKED — *may substitute linguini or spaghetti*

1/4 CUP BURGUNDY WINE — *may substitute any red wine*

1 TEASPOON RED ONION, MINCED

1 SPRIG FRESH TARRAGON — *or 1/4 teaspoon dry*

2 TABLESPOONS VEAL OR BEEF CONCENTRATE

1/8 TEASPOON SALT

1/8 TEASPOON BLACK PEPPER

1/4 CUP COLD BUTTER

### Cooking Instructions:

Fill a large pot with water, bring to a boil and cook pasta stirring occasionally until slightly firm. Drain under running cold water to cool and set aside.

Place a large sauté pan over high heat with all remaining ingredients (except butter). Cook sauce for about 2 minutes to reduce slightly.

Remove pan from heat and quickly stir in the cold butter.

Add the drained cooked pasta to the pan, toss to coat well.

Serve garnished with parsley if desired.

## TIP

*For a heartier meal add mushrooms, baked ham or even some leftover rotisserie chicken.*

# INDEX by Recipe

## SAUCES & GRAVIES •••

Fresh Salsa, 6
Fresh Tomato Sauce, 6
Demi-Glace, 7
Horseradish Demi-Glace, 8
Worcestershire Demi-Glace, 8
Madeira Wine Sauce, 8
Mushroom Bordelaise, 9
Cabernet Cream Sauce, 10
Bordelaise Sauce, 10
Alfredo Sauce, 11
Amaretto Sauce, 11
Béchamel Sauce, 12
Vodka Sauce, 13
Chicken Veloute, 14
Chablis Sauce, 15
Easy Cheesy Sauce, 15
Creamy Dijon Sauce, 16
Creamy Dill Sauce, 16
Roasted Red Pepper Vinaigrette, 16
Au Poivre Sauce, 17
Marsala Sauce, 17
Beef Au Jus, 18
Brown Gravy, 18
Chicken Gravy, 19
Holiday Turkey Gravy, 19

## SOUPS & STEWS ••••••

Stracciatella Soup, 22
Black Bean Soup, 23
Mushroom Florentine Soup, 24
Minestrone Soup with Tortellini, 25
Ground Beef Chili, 26
Cauliflower Soup, 27
Split Pea Soup, 27
...continued

*Soups & Stews continued...*

Taco Soup, 28
Easy Prep Chicken with Rice Soup, 29
Simply Chicken Stew, 29
Chuck Wagon Stew, 30
Egg Drop Soup, 30
Quick and Easy Italian Stew, 31
Hot and Sour Soup, 32
Chicken Tortilla Soup, 33

## BEEF ••••••••••••••••

Braised Short Ribs with Brussels
   Sprouts and Pearl Onions, 36
Beef and Broccoli, 37
Slow Cooked French Dip, 37
Fiesta Meatloaf, 38
Chicken Fried Steak, 38
Beef Stroganoff, 40
Slowed Cooked Hungarian Goulash, 41
Savory Grilled Beef Kabobs, 42
Steak Au Poivre, 43
Grilled Stuffed Burgers, 44
Simple Roast Beef Au Jus, 45
Italian Baked Meatballs, 46
Sirloin Chili Supreme, 47

## POULTRY ••••••••••••

Stuffed Chicken and
   Spinach Cannelloni, 50
Chicken Amaretto, 51
Chicken and Sausage Gumbo, 52
Tarragon Chicken, 53
Teriyaki Chicken, 54
Grilled Herb Chicken, 55
Slowed Cooked Tuscan Chicken, 56
Chicken Marsala, 57

# INDEX by Recipe

## PORK • • • • • • • • • • • • • •

Pulled Pork Sandwiches, 60

Pork Pot Roast, 61

Pork Loin Chops
with Apple & Sherry, 62

Pork Loin with Milk Gravy, 63

Two Can Cola Pork Roast, 64

Baby Back Ribs, 65

## VEAL & LAMB • • • • • • •

Roast Rack of Lamb
with Roasted Vegetables, 68

Braised Lamb Shanks
with Lemon and Mint, 69

Veal Francaise, 70

Veal Parmigiana, 71

Osso Buco, 72

Olive Infused Lamb Chops
with Red Wine, 73

## SEAFOOD • • • • • • • • • • • •

Lobster Newburg, 76

Shrimp with Rum Glaze, 77

Chicken, Sausage & Shrimp Paella, 78

Dilled Almond Trout, 79

Seared Salmon Supreme, 80

Shrimp Creole, 81

## BEANS & LEGUMES • • •

Italian White Bean Salad
with Sausage, 84

Black-Eyed Pea Salad
with Bacon & Bell Pepper, 85

Black Beans and Rice, 86

Curried Lentils, 87

...continued

*Beans & Legumes continued...*

Honey Baked Beans, 88

Buttery Lima Beans
with Sweet Bacon, 89

## VEGETABLES
## & SIDE DISHES • • • • • • •

Italian Chicken Spring Rolls, 92

Roasted Vegetables, 93

Ratatouille, 94

Portobella Mushroom with
Sundried Tomato Sauce, 95

Vegetable Quiche
with Bacon and Cheese, 96

Bacon Duxelle Stuffed Mushrooms, 97

## RICE & RISOTTO • • • • •

Cherry Tomato Risotto, 100

Wild Rice Almondine, 101

Portobella Risotto, 102

Risotto with
Gorgonzola and Walnuts, 103

Authentic Spanish Rice, 104

Chicken Rice Pilaf, 105

Couscous with
Pine Nuts and Raisins, 106

Asparagus Risotto, 107

## PASTA • • • • • • • • • • • • • •

Pasta Primavera, 110

Ratatouille Pasta, 111

Orzo Primavera, 112

Penne Alla Vodka, 113

Cheese Tortellini Alfredo
with Ham, 114

Angel Hair Pasta with Bordelaise
Butter Cream Sauce, 115

# GREAT FLAVORS
### STOCKS·SAUCES·SPICES

# INDEX by Concentrate

 BEEF

SAUCES & GRAVIES • • • • • • •
Demi-Glace, 7
Horseradish Demi-Glace, 8
Worcestershire Demi-Glace, 8
Madeira Wine Sauce, 8
Mushroom Bordelaise, 9
Bordelaise Sauce, 10
Au Poivre Sauce, 17
Marsala Sauce, 17
Beef Au Jus, 18
Brown Gravy, 18
Holiday Turkey Gravy, 19

SOUPS & STEWS • • • • • • • • •
Black Bean Soup, 23
Taco Soup, 28
Chuck Wagon Stew, 30
Quick and Easy Italian Stew, 31

BEEF • • • • • • • • • • • • • •
Braised Short Ribs with Brussels
    Sprouts and Pearl Onions, 36
Beef and Broccoli, 37
Slow Cooked French Dip, 37
Fiesta Meatloaf, 38
Chicken Fried Steak, 38
Beef Stroganoff, 40
Slowed Cooked Hungarian Goulash, 41
Savory Grilled Beef Kabobs, 42
Steak Au Poivre, 43
Grilled Stuffed Burgers, 44
Simple Roast Beef Au Jus, 45
Italian Baked Meatballs, 46
Sirloin Chili Supreme, 47

VEGETABLES & SIDE DISHES • •
Portobella Mushroom with
    Sundrided Tomato Sauce, 95

PASTA • • • • • • • • • • • • • •
Angel Hair Pasta with Bordelaise
    Butter Cream Sauce, 115

 CHICKEN

SAUCES & GRAVIES • • • • • • •
Alfredo Sauce, 11
Amaretto Sauce, 11
Béchamel Sauce, 12
Vodka Sauce, 13
Chicken Veloute, 14
Chablis Sauce, 15
Easy Cheesy Sauce, 15
Creamy Dijon Sauce, 16
Creamy Dill Sauce, 16
Chicken Gravy, 19

SOUPS & STEWS • • • • • • • • •
Stracciatella Soup, 22
Mushroom Florentine Soup, 24
Ground Beef Chili, 26
Cauliflower Soup, 27
Split Pea Soup, 27
Easy Prep Chicken with Rice Soup, 29
Simply Chicken Stew, 29
Egg Drop Soup, 30
Hot and Sour Soup, 32
Chicken Tortilla Soup, 33

POULTRY • • • • • • • • • • • • •
Stuffed Chicken and
    Spinach Cannelloni, 50
Chicken Amaretto, 51
Chicken and Sausage Gumbo, 52
Tarragon Chicken, 53
Teriyaki Chicken, 54
Grilled Herb Chicken, 55
Slowed Cooked Tuscan Chicken, 56
Chicken Marsala, 57

PORK • • • • • • • • • • • • • •
Pulled Pork Sandwiches, 60
Pork Pot Roast, 61
Pork Loin Chops
    with Apple & Sherry, 62
Pork Loin with Milk Gravy, 63

VEAL & LAMB • • • • • • • • • •
Braised Lamb Shanks
    with Lemon and Mint, 69
Veal Francaise, 70
Osso Buco, 72

*...continued on next page*

# INDEX by Concentrate continued...

*Chicken Concentrates continued...*

SEAFOOD • • • • • • • • • • •
Lobster Newburg, 76
Chicken, Sausage & Shrimp Paella, 78
Seared Salmon Supreme, 80
Shrimp Creole, 81

BEANS & LEGUMES • • • • • • •
Italian White Bean Salad w/ Sausage, 84
Black-Eyed Pea Salad
    with Bacon & Bell Pepper, 85
Black Beans and Rice, 86
Curried Lentils, 87

VEGETABLES & SIDE DISHES • •
Italian Chicken Spring Rolls, 92
Bacon Duxelle Stuffed Mushrooms, 97

RICE & RISOTTO • • • • • • • •
Cherry Tomato Risotto, 100
Wild Rice Almondine, 101
Authentic Spanish Rice, 104
Chicken Rice Pilaf, 105

## MUSHROOM

SAUCES & GRAVIES • • • • • • •
Mushroom Bordelaise, 9

SOUPS & STEWS • • • • • • • • •
Mushroom Florentine Soup, 24

VEGETABLES & SIDE DISHES • •
Bacon Duxelle Stuffed Mushrooms, 97

## SEAFOOD

SEAFOOD • • • • • • • • • • • •
Lobster Newburg, 76

## VEAL

SAUCES & GRAVIES • • • • • • •
Demi-Glace, 7
Horseradish Demi-Glace, 8
Worcestershire Demi-Glace, 8
Madeira Wine Sauce, 8
Mushroom Bordelaise, 9
Au Poivre Sauce, 17
Marsala Sauce, 17

## VEGETABLE

SAUCES & GRAVIES • • • • • • •
Fresh Salsa, 6
Fresh Tomato Sauce, 6
Mushroom Bordelaise, 9
Roasted Red Pepper Vinaigrette, 16

SOUPS & STEWS • • • • • • • • •
Minestrone Soup with Tortellini, 25

BEEF • • • • • • • • • • • • • •
Slowed Cooked Hungarian Goulash, 41

PORK • • • • • • • • • • • • • •
Pork Loin Chops w/ Apple & Sherry, 62
Two Can Cola Pork Roast, 64
Baby Back Ribs, 65

VEAL & LAMB • • • • • • • • • •
Roast Rack of Lamb
    with Roasted Vegetables, 68
Veal Parmigiana, 71
Olive Infused Lamb Chops
    with Red Wine, 73

SEAFOOD • • • • • • • • • • • •
Shrimp with Rum Glaze, 77
Dilled Almond Trout, 79

BEANS & LEGUMES • • • • • • •
Italian White Bean Salad w/ Sausage, 84
Honey Baked Beans, 88
Buttery Lima Beans w/ Sweet Bacon, 89

VEGETABLES & SIDE DISHES • •
Roasted Vegetables, 93
Ratatouille, 94
Vegetable Quiche w/ Bacon and Cheese, 96

RICE & RISOTTO • • • • • • • •
Portobella Risotto, 102
Risotto w/ Gorgonzola and Walnuts, 103
Couscous w/ Pine Nuts and Raisins, 106
Asparagus Risotto, 107

PASTA • • • • • • • • • • • • •
Pasta Primavera, 110
Ratatouille Pasta, 111
Orzo Primavera, 112
Penne Alla Vodka, 113
Cheese Tortellini Alfredo w/ Ham, 114

# TIP

*eat well & enjoy!*